Paul Martin is an award-winning, v. ──── ───── ──────── ────────
mixologist, trainer and motivational speaker. During his
bartending career, he has set two world speed-cocktail-mixing
records and won seven global mixology titles. He runs some of the
most sought-after bartender and hospitality training courses and
has trained more than 50,000 bartenders in more than twenty-five
countries around the world. Paul has appeared in his role of
'cocktail expert' on TV and radio on many occasions including for
three full series on Food Network Daily in the 1990s. Paul is also
an accomplished motivational speaker and can often be found
delivering talks on human connection, communication skills and
other human interaction topics. His TEDx Talk on how he used
his knowledge of sign language to develop a new technique for
improving people's body-language skills has received more than
500,000 views on YouTube.

ULTIMATE
BARTENDING

LEARN THE SKILLS AND TECHNIQUES
OF THE WORLD'S TOP BARTENDERS
AND COCKTAIL MIXOLOGISTS

PAUL MARTIN

ROBINSON

ROBINSON

First published in Great Britain in 2017 by
Robinson

Copyright © Paul Martin, 2017

10 9 8 7 6 5 4 3 2 1

A CIP catalogue record for this book
is available from the British Library.

ISBN: 978-1-47213-981-8

Typeset by Mousemat Design Limited

Printed and bound in Great Britain by
Clays Ltd, St Ives plc

Papers used by Robinson are from
well-managed forests and other responsible
sources.

MIX
Paper from
responsible sources
FSC® C104740

Robinson
An imprint of
Little, Brown Book Group
Carmelite House
50 Victoria Embankment
London EC4Y 0DZ

An Hachette UK Company
www.hachette.co.uk

www.littlebrown.co.uk

How To Books are published by Robinson,
an imprint of Little, Brown Book Group. We
welcome proposals from authors who have
first-hand experience of their subjects.
Please set out the aims of your book, its
target market and its suggested contents in
an email to Nikki.Read@howtobooks.co.uk

Contents

Introduction: The DNA of an Ultimate Bartender   ix

CHAPTER **1**   **Laying the Foundations for Ultimate Bartending**   **1**

Achieving consistency   3

Delivering the perfect serve   3

Nailing the final serve   6

Adding the little extras   7

Mixing cocktails   9

Mastering the three fundamental mixing methods   10

CHAPTER **2**   **ABL (Always Be Learning)**   **17**

Opportunities for learning   20

Learning from your colleagues   22

Running your own skills sessions   23

Reviewing your guest interactions   23

Setting goals and targets based on specific techniques   24

Arranging distillery visits   26

Joining online groups/message boards   27

Introducing awards and incentives   28

Buying materials (like this book)   28

Setting yourself daily learning/sharing goals   28

Visiting other bars (not to get drunk, to see how
they do things)   29

Stepping outside your industry to see how others do it   29

CHAPTER **3**   **Being Part of the A-Team: The whole is greater
than the sum of the parts**   **33**

The ultimate goal of the Ultimate Bartender   34

Building relationships   35

Developing a reciprocal environment (reciprocity)   36
Building rapport   38

CHAPTER
4   **The Amazing Benefits of 2 vs 1**   **41**
Showing a 'tell'   41
Two compared to one   43
Making the transition to two hands   46
Mixing spirits and mixers   48
Mixing cocktails   49

CHAPTER
5   **Upselling Guests Beyond Their Expectations**   **53**
The bar-industry advantage   54
Grasping the Second Serve opportunity   59
Asking the question!   60
Getting the timing right   61
Remembering the sound of opportunity   63
Styles of recommendation   64
Recommendation tips   67

CHAPTER
6   **Possessing an Attitude to Serve**   **73**
My 'one-trick-pony' chef   75
Just be yourself. Is this really the best advice?   76
Three tips to achieving an attitude to serve   78

CHAPTER
7   **Becoming a 'Heads Up' Ultimate Bartender**   **81**
Attendance up but heads down!   82
It's not how long it takes that matters, it's how long it feels   84
From hell to heaven in one night   85
Communication: The hidden super-power   87
Becoming a 'heads up' Ultimate Bartender   90

CHAPTER 8	**Reading the Guests and Taking Control**	**97**
	Considering age	98
	Thinking about gender	99
	Being influenced by group size	99
	Profiling group types	100
	Watching the clock: Time of day	100
	Watching the clock: Day of the week	101
	Watching the calendar: Seasons	102
	Looking out for personal occasions	104
	Celebrating universal occasions	104
	Observing a guest's dress style	105
CHAPTER 9	**Living the Mantra, Knowledge is Bartending Power**	**109**
	Taking responsibility for your own development	110
	All it takes is ten minutes a week	113
	Visiting the producers	115
	Becoming a bit geeky!	117
	Been there, seen it, done very little!	118
CHAPTER 10	**Connecting with Guests and Influencing their Decisions**	**121**
	Selling the sizzle	122
	Understanding the role of the limbic system	123
	Albert Mehrabian's communication model	125
	It's not what you say, it's the way that you say it (and project it)	127
	Body talk	130
	Avoiding communication conflict	131
	Perfectly communicating a recommendation	132
	Using reciprocity as a tool for great service	134
	Powerless to resist	135
	I wouldn't have done that!	137

CHAPTER 11 **Understanding that It's Never Personal** 143

Just another opportunity to demonstrate your skills 146

It's not the real you 147

Easier said than done 149

Thinking like an actor 149

Using empathy 151

How empathetic are you? 152

How do people make empathy work for them? 156

Realising that It's All in the Mind 161

CHAPTER 12 What is stress? 161

Living in the future 162

Wise words on perspective 164

The Power of Now 166

Performing: The Theatre of Bartending 169

CHAPTER 13 Projecting your stance 171

Checking and holding glasses 171

Pouring (jigger or free) 172

Shaking 173

Communicating through dress sense 175

Interacting with your team 175

A word on avoiding arrogance 176

A word on flair bartending 178

All the Bar's a Stage: The Big Show 181

CHAPTER 13 Hanging! 182

The Ultimate Waitress 183

Same place, different experience 185

It's all about the service 187

Index 190

The DNA of an Ultimate Bartender

Contrary to popular belief, mixing and serving great drinks barely scratches the surface of the characteristics and skills that define a world-class bartender. In order to become truly great at what you do, you first need to understand the multitude of interpersonal skills, techniques and abilities that are brought to bear by the very best of the mixology industry. Whether you are a bar owner, manager or individual bartender, in this book, I will help you to understand those skills and help you to become the Ultimate Bartender.

....

So, if you had to rank yourself out of 10 as a bartender, what score would you award yourself? Interestingly, whatever score you have decided upon, I can tell you that it is almost certainly not a true reflection of your abilities but more a case of how you rank yourself against what you perceive to be a perfect 10. It's all about perception. In all the years that I have been running bartender training courses and seminars, people rarely, if ever, are able to accurately rate their abilities in the context of what the perfect bartender actually looks like. This is ultimately because their view of perfection is limited by their own experiences. They may be striving for perfection, but only their own personal view of perfection. Indeed, when we set ourselves limits, those limits in turn define the levels to which we progress.

If you have ever been into a gymnasium, you see this phenomenon in action. A guy who has decided to get fit walks in to a gym on day one and among other things notices a rack of dumbbells ranging in weight from 1kg through to 20kg, rising in 1kg increments. In trying to establish a good weight with which to start training he picks up the middle weight of 10kg and gives it a go. Depending upon how he gets on, he may decide that he needs to start with something a little lighter, or possibly a bit heavier, but eventually he will settle upon his starting weight. Over the coming weeks and months as his fitness and strength develop, he will gradually increase the weight with the ultimate goal being to work up to the limit, the big 20kg dumbbells. In fact, psychologically, 20kg becomes the summit, the final goal, the target that he will strive for. It also becomes his perceived limit. In time, he may not get to 20kg but he will certainly improve. Possibly reaching an impressive 18kg.

However, had that same guy walked in to a different gymnasium on day one and found that the dumbbells in the second gym began at 5kg and went up to 50kg he would have achieved very different targets. In this case, his perception of the summit would be much higher (50kg) and as a consequence he would have that higher goal as his motivation for development and improvement. Over time his level of improvement would not be limited by the 20kg goal established in the first gymnasium, and as a consequence, while most people would not get anywhere near the level of strength required to use 50kg dumbbells, he would almost certainly exceed the 20kg weight that he would likely fail to achieve in the first gym.

In fact, in tests, it has been demonstrated that people consistently achieve greater gains when exposed to the second scenario as opposed to the first. When their perceptions of limits change! And this phenomenon is repeated time and again throughout every aspect of our lives. Join a table tennis club where the members are all national-standard players and your level of play will develop much faster and to a higher standard than if you had joined a local club with average players. Join the best music school in the country, surrounded by some of the country's finest talent, and you will become a better pianist than had you simply remained at a standard comprehensive school under the tutelage of the local music teacher. Work with the most highly skilled bartenders in the world and you will become a much finer bartender than had you simply worked in an average bar alongside low-skilled mixologists.

And just to be clear, this is not simply because you are being exposed to greater skills; it's because your view of what is achievable is far greater and therefore you are not limited in your own development by restricted perceptions of what is achievable.

My job as a trainer is not simply to improve a bartender's skills but, more importantly, to change their perceptions of what perfection could actually be. You'll never reach the summit if you fail to realise that it's beyond the cloud line.

So, let's think about how you may score yourself right now. Imagine that your view of the perfect bartender was someone who could pull a pint of beer, tell the difference between a red and white wine and was able to mix five different cocktails from memory, then you could quite easily give yourself an 8 if you could do 80 per cent of that. However, if your view of the perfect bartender was someone who had amazing product knowledge to the extent that he could mix more than 1,000 perfectly served cocktails from memory, could identify any wine, including the year, from a blind taste, was an amazing communicator, an entertaining host, etc., you may then consider yourself a 2 based on the fact that you are 20 per cent of the way to achieving that level of expertise. However, out of the two scenarios, which one is probably the better bartender? The one who scored himself an 8 or the one who scored himself a 2?

And consider this also: the one who scored an 8 is also under the impression that he only needs a small improvement to become the perfect bartender. After all, based on his own perceptions of perfection he is already 80 per cent of the way there. On the other hand, not only is the bartender who scored himself a 2 probably a better bartender already, he can also see that there is a far greater opportunity for development and improvement based on the fact that he has ranked himself so low. In this scenario, not only has he already surpassed the first bartender, but based on his very different perceptions of perfection, he will continue to strive to improve long after bartender number one has decided there is nothing else he needs to know!

As a consequence, the key to becoming an *Ultimate* Bartender is first being able to see what skills and knowledge the perfect 10 is likely to display and then to mark yourself in relation to that. Not simply to score yourself based on your own impression.

Therefore, if, through this book, I am going to help you on your way to becoming the very finest bartender you could become, I'm first going to have to change your view of what that looks like.

So, what skills in my opinion does the Ultimate Bartender possess? First and foremost, he or she would need to be a great communicator and people person. In my experience, the world's most engaging and entertaining bartenders don't necessarily mix the best drinks. Or, if they do happen to mix great drinks, that is far from the main appeal for their guests. However, an ability to connect with their guests, build instant rapport, demonstrate empathy, expertly use humour, express themselves both passionately and articulately, take their guests on an unexpected journey, and communicate across the age ranges, gender types and social and cultural groups is the absolute cornerstone of everything that they do. It lays the foundations for every element of the Ultimate Bartender's craft and in doing so opens their guests up to a service experience beyond anything they have become accustomed to.

The Ultimate Bartender has a service mindset and is always seeking to exceed his guests' expectations. There is a thirst (pun!) for knowledge that drives continual improvement throughout their career. At no stage does the Ultimate Bartender rest on his laurels. He has an innate understanding of the power of teamwork and is never motivated by self-promotion or ego. In fact, our Ultimate Bartender thrives on an ability to contribute to a team dynamic and help to bring out the best of himself by helping others to get the best from themselves.

Our Ultimate Bartender is able to work at speed and with efficiency, without it detracting from his main focus, connecting and engaging with his guests. To this end, his head is always 'up' with his eyes on the game. In fact, eye contact is one of his major weapons in the delivery of great service: with it he is able to read the guests and gather information that he skilfully uses to help develop rapport. He has a perspective on his guests that allows him to engage with them and redirect their experiences, enabling them to experience drinks and combinations they would never have discovered without him. He is a skilled influencer with a grasp of the psychology of decision-making. As a result, he's able to influence decisions in the guests' favour, helping them to overcome any lingering insecurities about experimentation and new experiences.

He's the perfect professional, able to separate the professional self from the personal self. This empowers him to deal with negative situations, challenging guests or general 'bad days' in a considered, service-orientated manner. He doesn't get personally involved or upset; he becomes professionally engaged, viewing every negative as an opportunity to develop a more profound positive. Likewise, our Ultimate Bartender has the tools and understanding to identify the triggers for stress and then employ techniques to help dissipate that very stress. He's empathetic in a fundamental way, understanding situations from the perspective of someone who wants to understand, rather than defend an opposing position, and as a result is an expert in connecting with the most demanding of guests.

Bartending for the Ultimate Bartender is more than a service: it is entertainment, which can be seen in the way he holds himself, handles the equipment, pours a glass of wine, shakes a cocktail or even stands. By doing so, he feeds into the involuntary response of guests who experience this level of bartending supremacy and who in turn lead to the spreading of his reputation. Our Ultimate Bartender is not afraid to accept that he is human and fallible but also understands that he has this in common with all of his guests, and by delivery of Ultimate Bartending standards is more likely to be supported by them when busy or if something were to go wrong. For our Ultimate Bartender, all the world is a stage and he continues to do everything in his power to make his stage show the most impressive his guests have experienced.

And of course, they will continue to develop and hone their drink mixing/serving skills so that their delivery of exceptional service is indeed brought to fruition through the vehicle of a fabulous drink. This is our perfect 10, our *Ultimate Bartender*.

Now mark yourself against this. Where are you now? If you are honest with yourself you will have marked yourself much lower than when I posed this question at the opening of this chapter. But whatever mark you have awarded yourself, consider that to be your starting point. In the chapters that follow I will introduce you to the skills and techniques that will enable you to climb the Ultimate Bartending ladder. And while you won't become a perfect 10 overnight, you will be on the right track to achieving that immense perfect 10 goal. And as you do so, remember this: If you only become a 4 or 5 on this new scale, you will almost certainly be well in excess of a 10 on any regular bartender's scale and will be delivering to your guests an experience far beyond that enjoyed by the vast majority. Thereafter, you can simply continue to hone your skills until you reach the summit you seek.

CHAPTER 1

Laying the Foundations for Ultimate Bartending

This chapter addresses the importance of mixing and serving great drinks from the perspective of laying the foundations on which to further build your skills.

While mixing great drinks tends to be the sole focus of many bartenders, for the top performers, the standard of drinks is seen as the foundation upon which they build their other skills. It sets the tone for the service experience. In itself, mixing great drinks is about bringing a range of practical skills to bear on your approach to every libation, whether it's a glass of mineral water or a sophisticated cocktail. Here we will outline and define the approach required to get you on the right track to establishing a solid foundation from which to deliver your amazing service experience.

....

I know some truly great bartenders. I also know some incredibly skilled drink-makers. And yet it's not always the case that the second group are able to deliver an exceptional guest experience. Neither is it a given that the first group necessarily mix the best drinks. In fact, some of the best drinks that I have experienced have been mixed by a couple of the most unengaging characters that I have ever seen working a bar. In truth, their self-obsessed sense of importance ruined the entire experience for me and left me with no desire to visit their bars again. However, it's also true to say that a number of my most memorable and enjoyable experiences have been delivered by incredibly engaging bartenders who mixed decidedly average drinks. In these cases, I have always been happy to return, regardless of the drink quality. I simply enjoyed myself so much.

> **It's also true to say that a number of my most memorable and enjoyable experiences have been delivered by incredibly engaging bartenders who mixed decidedly average drinks.**

The point I am making here is that quality of service, engagement and entertainment is far more valuable in the eye of the guest than the skill of mixing great drinks. And yet, when it comes to the very finest bartenders they realise one important fact: these skills are not mutually exclusive. That they can live in perfect harmony, with one embellishing the experience of the other, resulting in the delivery of the Ultimate Bartending experience for their guests.

Indeed, this is one of the characteristics of the Ultimate Bartender. They assign equal importance to both elements of their bartending skills. Why be good at one, at the expense of another? Why not mix the finest drinks possible, all wrapped up in an unsurpassed service experience? View the skill of mixing great drinks as the foundation of your craft rather than the entirety of it.

So, in this section I am going to share a number of tips and directions to help you develop your drink-making skills and lay the foundations on which to continue building.

Achieving consistency

Being consistent is the sign of a great drink-maker. There is nothing worse than enjoying a drink, ordering another and it being even slightly different to the first one. Whether it's a simple spirit and mixer, a pint of beer, a glass of wine or a sophisticated cocktail, once you have established a standard you need to be able to replicate it time and again. Make no mistake, if there are differences your guests will spot them. You need to consider every drink-making action so that nothing is random.

Delivering the perfect serve

This is the principle of trying to serve each drink perfectly, at its zenith, so that it couldn't be any better. In this regard, it is important to establish precisely what your perfect serve standards are. You are looking to create a defined set of standards for each of your drink types or categories. In terms of categories think beer, wine, spirits (straight), spirit and mixer, cocktails, etc. It's worth remembering that we charge significantly more for a drink than it would cost our guests if they made it for themselves at home. In some cases, it's dozens of times more, and so we need to ask ourselves, 'What are they getting from us that they don't get at home?' And is what they are receiving value for money?

As we progress through this book, we will address all the other elements of Ultimate Bartending service that impact the overall sense of value for money. But for now, with specific regard to the drink itself, we need to consider the following:

Using the perfect glass

I'm a great believer that the style of glass that you serve a drink in influences the guest's perception of its quality. For example, consider the timeless beauty of a classic martini cocktail served in an iconic martini-style glass. The clarity of the gin and vermouth mixture displayed in a sublime conical glass with a speared olive conjures images of class and sophistication. And yet, if you served the same 75ml of liquid in a pint glass it would be an entirely different proposition. It's easy to see how the experience of the drink could be quite different. So, which glass do you use for which drink? Think about the drink type and ask yourself how enticing it looks. Challenge yourself to 'frame' your drinks so they look desirable and once you have selected your glasses make sure you stick with them. For example, if it's a 12oz highball for a G&T, make sure it always is. Don't get lazy and serve it in a 10oz highball or a 12oz rocks. It just looks unprofessional and demonstrates a lack of care in the bartender's attitude.

Understanding the importance of ice

Think about ice. We use ice to keep our drinks cold. The more ice you use, the colder the drink remains and the less it dilutes. Remember: ice keeps itself colder for longer and it's always battling against the slightly warmer temperature of the drink. If you use less ice, the temperature of the drink itself will overpower the temperature of the ice and it will melt faster, hence diluting the drink quicker. So, decide how much ice is the perfect amount for your drinks (usually between three quarters to a full glass) and make sure it's the same every time. Also, if you serve your ice from ice buckets rather than ice chests, make sure you continually drain the old ice and keep it topped up. Nothing's worse than putting half-melted ice into a drink along with the water that gathers at the bottom of the bucket.

> **Nothing's worse than putting half-melted ice into a drink along with the water that gathers at the bottom of the bucket.**

Garnishing your drinks

We use garnishes in drinks for a number of reasons. Firstly, for aesthetics. It makes the drink look pretty and of a higher quality. Next, it adds flavour (if dropped into the drink), and finally aroma, especially if it sits atop the drink or glass. Whether it's a wedge of lime in a G&T or something more elaborate for a cocktail, give it the attention it deserves. Keep the garnishes uniform and of the same quality, making sure they are fresh. If using fruit and it is old or dry, just don't use it. Also, don't be mean when cutting fruit into pieces. You should be getting six wedges from a lime and not twelve plus. Trying to make a piece of fruit stretch too far communicates a clear message to the guest. Namely, that you are more focused on saving as many pennies as you can than thinking about making the drink the highest quality possible.

When storing pre-cut garnishes, keep them dry and preferably chilled, definitely in airtight containers. This will keep them at their optimum throughout the shift. DO NOT LET THEM SIT IN WATER. This washes away all flavour and aroma and results in them turning soggy! And finally, at the end of a shift, if there are any pre-cut garnishes remaining THROW THEM AWAY. There is nothing that you can do to store them overnight and have them remain fresh and fragrant the next day. You should be preparing new, fresh garnishes every day, ideally for every shift. Even better, in an ideal world (I know what you're thinking: 'Who lives in an ideal world?') you would prepare them fresh each time you mixed a drink!

Nailing the final serve

Have you ever been in to a fast-food restaurant, seen the images of perfectly formed, symmetrical burgers layered with vibrant juicy tomatoes, dollops of 'special' sauce and a slice of geometrically perfect cheese melted *'en pointe'*? Have you then ordered one only to discover that in reality, when your burger arrives, it looks like it had been dropped on the floor just before being packaged? Yes? That's because advertisers and marketing companies are employed to sell the dream, to create imagery that represents (in this case) the burger in its perfect incarnation, so that you buy in to the offer of perfection. Of course, the reality is somewhat different!

However, in the bar industry, the Ultimate Bartender has a distinct advantage over his burger-producing cousin. Because, with the correct care and attention, by simply bringing all the above considerations together, he is able to produce real-life drinks of perfection that accurately mirror the imagery that the most creative marketers can produce for advertising campaigns.

Take for example the iconic poster image of a Gordon's gin and tonic. It is an image that has been used to promote their brand the world over. It's a tall, clean 12oz highball glass, it is filled with ice, has a measure of gin topped with tonic and filled to within 10mm of the top of the glass (note that it is not served half-poured with the tonic by the side waiting for you, the guest, to finish it off yourself), and is garnished with a freshly cut wedge of lime. In fact, it is everything that I have mentioned in the steps above. So, you see, there is no reason why our drinks can't look like iconic poster images. In fact, if they don't look as good, it's just a missed opportunity and has nothing to do with the image being an unachievable fantasy and everything to do with the amount of care and attention you apply to your drink-making.

Adding the little extras

It's funny how the small things can make the biggest difference. In terms of a guest's perception of drink quality, this is certainly the case. Using the above G&T as an example: if you served the identical drink but without the freshly cut lime wedge and you then lined them up next to one another, the drink with the garnish would appear far more appealing than the one without. Likewise, if one drink had a freshly cut garnish and the other had a slightly dry, pithy, more thinly cut garnish.

With this in mind, it's worth considering what else we can do to elevate the appeal and presentation of our drinks. Consider this: adding a straw, preferably a black one as it feels more sophisticated, will also change the appearance and perceived quality of the serve, as will serving your drinks on bev naps (beverage napkins). Likewise, if your budget stretches, you can also consider investing in higher-quality glassware. Maybe you can find a style and design that enables you to create your own signature serve for the G&T.

Ultimately, whether you are selling your G&Ts for a few pounds in a local pub or you are charging the extraordinary prices that top venues and hotels appear to get away with, you will be using the same ingredients. The pub's brand of gin is the same as the five-star hotel's; the pub's ice is made from frozen water just like the hotel's; if they serve the same brand then their tonics are identical; and both venues' limes grow on trees. So, ultimately, it is the little touches that make the difference: the

> **The pub's brand of gin is the same as the five-star hotel's; the pub's ice is made from frozen water just like the hotel's.**

care, the attention to detail, the focus on consistency and the little extras.

Mixing cocktails

While technique is important for all styles of drink service, it is of particular importance when it comes to mixology (creating cocktails). There are so many aspects to consider when producing a range of cocktails that it's easy to understand how practising and mastering the various techniques will stand you in good stead as you expand your knowledge of recipes and drink styles. I always advise bartenders that it's not the number of recipes that you commit to memory that counts but how well you can turn those recipes into amazing cocktails.

My very first cocktail bartending job, thirty something years ago, was a case in point. The bar had a fairly extensive cocktail list numbering over 150 cocktail recipes. Before I could start working on the bar I had to commit each one of them to memory! However, once I began serving, my lack of technique and experience resulted in me serving a lot of very average cocktails (and that's being generous). You see, without the fundamental mixing skills, simply knowing what went into the drink meant that I was riding somewhat blind. It was a bit like being given some flour, water, tomatoes and mozzarella and being asked to make an amazing pizza! No technique, no chance! It wasn't until I changed jobs and worked in a bar where the main focus was technique, making a small selection of great cocktails, that I really started to understand what producing amazing drinks was all about.

With this in mind, here are a few tips that have underpinned everything I have gone on to achieve throughout my career, both as a bartender and then subsequently as a trainer.

Mastering the three fundamental mixing methods
Shaking

Ever wondered why we shake some cocktails and not others? Well, the process of shaking a cocktail is quite full on. It rapidly mixes and chills the ingredients, but as a result of the high-impact coming together of the ice, it also dilutes them very quickly. This is the perfect technique for producing many cocktails, allowing us to mix, chill and dilute at speed. But while a major aspect of being able to shake well is controlling dilution, it tends to be too aggressive for the more subtle and delicately balanced cocktails where we need to retain much greater control than is achievable when shaking. The general rule for shaking is to do so fast and hard – no rocking it to sleep! The aim is to get the ingredients to combine effectively while lowering the temperature. Dilution is very much part of the final mixture as far as shaken cocktails are concerned, but as with any other ingredient you need to know how much you are adding. Too much (or too little) water will inevitably impact the balance of the final drink.

So how long should you shake for? Again, it depends. How vigorous is your shaking technique? For me, I shake fairly hard, which means that a cosmopolitan cocktail only needs four to five seconds in my shaker. For other less 'enthusiastic' bartenders it may require seven to eight seconds. To some degree, this is something you need to discover for yourself. Practise, check, practise again! Also, ingredients can influence the shake time. For example, if I am using cream I shake a little longer, egg white even longer still (to get the white smooth and frothy). When it comes to juice, I shake pineapple juice for slightly less time than orange because the pineapple froths a lot whereas the orange froths hardly at all. Ultimately, don't think of the shake as something you do the same way every time. Try to understand the drink, what you are trying to achieve as a final result, and develop and refine your technique accordingly.

> **Ultimately, don't think of the shake as something you do the same way every time.**

Stirring

When we stir a cocktail, we are endeavouring to achieve the same goal as when shaking. Namely to mix, chill and dilute. However, as explained above, when we stir we have much greater control over the dilution. Generally, when stirring a cocktail, we take much longer than when shaking. This way we can gradually assess how well the drink is blending and chilling, and ultimately, by eye, check the dilution. On the whole, it tends to be the classic style of cocktails that are stirred. Martinis, manhattans, etc. These are drinks that are usually a combination of spirits, vermouths, liqueurs and so on, but which are less likely to include the heavier ingredients that would more likely require shaking. My recommended technique is to fill your mixing glass with ice, add the ingredients and, using a bar spoon, stir in rapid smooth circles. You are looking for the ice to revolve smoothly around the glass and not clatter about.

Building

A built drink is one that is made directly in the glass. This can be something as simple as a G&T as mentioned earlier, or a more elaborate cocktail such as a mojito. In the case of built drinks, all the blending (if required), chilling, etc. happens as the drink is being constructed. It is important when getting to know your built drinks that you understand which ingredients are added in what order, whether there are any actions that need to take place along the way (stirring for example) and what the final drink is intended to look like. This will help guide you in terms of confidently constructing your drinks and ensuring that you serve fantastic examples of them consistently.

Let's take the mojito as an example. The recipe is simple: rum, fresh mint, lime juice, sugar, soda. However, the process is somewhat more convoluted. Here's the method that Bacardi recommends for its 'original' mojito.

> Start by squeezing the juice of 1 lime in to a 12–14oz tall glass, add 2 bar spoons of caster sugar (or adjust to taste) and give a little stir to help some of the sugar dissolve. Now take 6–8 fresh mint leaves, give them a slap in your hands (to help release the mint oils) and add to the glass. Once again give the mixture a small stir to help the flavours release and

combine. Now half-fill the glass with crushed ice, add the rum (approximately 50ml) and churn the mixture together. Now we are helping to combine the flavours and chill the drink. The reason we only add half a glass of ice at this stage is so the drink is easier to 'churn'.

Next bring the level of crushed ice to within 10mm of the top of the glass (the level of the drink will rise along with the ice) and give the mixture another stir. Finally, add a splash of soda, add more crushed ice to create a 'peak' and garnish by tucking a sprig of mint (pre-slapped) into the top. Add a straw to the drink, nestled against the mint garnish (this is so you get the maximum aroma from the mint while you drink) and serve!

As you can see, this drink is all about process, order, technique and final coherent result. It is the perfect example of why Ultimate Bartenders work on developing their building skills and why their drinks are so much more enjoyable than those where building has meant no more than chucking everything in the glass and giving it a quick stir (if you're lucky)!

> **This drink is all about process, order, technique and final coherent result.**

There are of course acres of text on producing and mixing drinks and I have merely skimmed over a few essential techniques and considerations here. The main reason for this is that this is not a book about mixing drinks. I have made an assumption that every reader of this book will already have attained a certain level of drink-making skill – and what we are concentrating on are the skills and techniques that will help develop the drink-makers into fully rounded bartenders, eventually *Ultimate Bartenders*. There are countless books, videos and courses available for those of you that are still looking to improve on your cocktail-making abilities (I have produced a number myself), but this is about becoming a supremely talented bartender and therefore we will leave the drink-making behind now and move on to the sexy stuff...

TAKEAWAYS FROM THIS CHAPTER

- Consistency is key. Always make sure that no matter how many times you mix a drink, it is exactly the same each time.

- Deliver the perfect serve. Every element of mixing your drink should be carried out to its maximum potential so that it couldn't be mixed any better.

- Apply the same dedication and attention to detail whatever the drink. Whether you are serving a bottle of mineral water or a sophisticated cocktail, you should be looking to achieve a level of service that is unsurpassable.

- Perfect your cocktail-mixing techniques. By understanding the processes and performing them correctly, your cocktails will be of a higher standard across the board.

- Always remember the 'little extras'. They can often make the biggest differences in terms of your guests' perception of quality and value.

CHAPTER 2

ABL (Always Be Learning)

This chapter considers the value of knowledge and how to embrace and benefit from a learning mindset.

An ability and willingness to continually develop as a professional is a key characteristic of the Ultimate Bartender. The mindset is about continually striving to deliver an ever-improving guest experience. In other words, bringing more tools to the table. Looking for opportunities, continually challenging yourselves, keeping an eye on industry developments, watching and learning from co-workers, learning from experiences (good and bad) and always endeavouring to view the service experience from the perspective of the guest. Here we examine how a learning mindset can be integrated in to the daily routine and how to take every opportunity to expand your knowledge and experience.

....

For more than thirty years I have watched the *Mastermind* quiz programme on the BBC. For those of you unfamiliar with it, it is a British quiz show famous for its challenging questions, intimidating setting and air of seriousness. Contestants take part in two rounds of questioning, the first being on a 'specialist subject' chosen by the contestant and the second a general-knowledge round. The programme was devised by Bill Wright, who drew inspiration from his experiences of being interrogated by the Gestapo during the Second World War.

While I am by no means one of the world's deepest fonts of knowledge, I would suggest that I have a reasonable depth, especially when it comes to knowledge of the general kind. Nevertheless, the main attraction of this programme has always resided in the depth of knowledge the contestants exhibit in relation to their chosen 'specialist subject'. For me, taking my regular place in front of the TV, the challenge lies not in how many of their specialist questions I can answer, but whether I can answer any of them at all. In all the years I have been watching, I don't think I have scored higher than 3 or 4 (out of 20 or so) in any of the hundreds of specialist rounds I have played along with.

And then, one evening, completely without warning, my moment arrived. The contestant sat in the famous black chair, gave his name, and then when asked what his 'specialist subject' was, answered, 'The Whiskies of Scotland'.

I sat bolt upright, rolled up my sleeves and called my wife to come and witness my performance. Because, after quarter of a century of having watched this show, I was suddenly faced with a subject that I know a lot about. Whisky is one of my strong subjects: I have been training people on it for years, I have visited many dozens of

I sat bolt upright, rolled up my sleeves and called my wife to come and witness my performance.

distilleries, picked the brains of countless head distillers, read extensively on the subject, attended more tasting sessions than I can count, and have enjoyed the company of like-minded whisky enthusiasts for the majority of my adult life. Not to mention (I'm going to anyway) that I have my own collection of more than 150 whiskies (mostly drinkers, a few keepers), of which I partake on a far-too-regular basis. Yes, if ever there was a subject for me to excel in this was it. This was my moment.

I settled back, wife by my side ready to be suitably impressed, and the clock started: two minutes, questions coming in quick-fire succession ... history, characters, distillation, styles, geography, each one falling within a sub-category of which I had extensive knowledge. And then it was done. The two minutes were up. The contestant did pretty well, scoring an admirable 15 out of the 19 questions he was asked. And me? I scored 2. Just 2! My wife got to her feet, looked at me and said, 'Someone needs to go back to school.' And with that she left the room, leaving me to re-evaluate the level of knowledge I thought I possessed.

You see, when it comes to knowledge in any subject, whether (as in my case) it is whisky, or accountancy or opera or absolutely anything, no matter how much you may know, there is always someone who knows more than you... and there is probably someone who knows more than them, too. The fact is that, in your quest to become an Ultimate Bartender, it is not enough to be the most knowledgeable person in the room (or your bar); it is about becoming the most knowledgeable that you can possibly be. Every Ultimate Bartender understands this basic fact and as a result they are always hungry to learn, always striving to improve, always understanding that the more they learn the less they realise they actually know, which in turn feeds their desire for professional development even further. It is the Ultimate Bartender's perpetual circle.

If you look around and you are the smartest person in the room, you're in the wrong room.
Anon

Opportunities for learning

Let's first consider the general opportunities to learn, the ones that most of us are aware of. If you are fortunate, the company that you work for has some form of internal training programme in place, something that all employees are exposed to. Outside of this you can always take the opportunity to get in the drinks brands to run training courses. The benefit of these (from the company's point of view) is that the training is funded by the drinks brand providing it. However, the downside is that there is an understandable lean towards the drinks brand's own products and therefore you don't get the completely dispassionate, non-partisan approach that you would from an independent trainer. Then of course there are specialist independent trainers (like myself), although many smaller companies are put off by the fact they will have to dip in to their own funds to finance such training.

However, if you simply rely on the above, you will be missing a huge opportunity and relying solely on your employer to dictate your level of skill development. It's a lazy approach! One of the things we discover on the road to becoming an Ultimate Bartender is that the very best ones take ownership of their development, taking every opportunity to improve their knowledge and develop their skills. And as with most things, the opportunities for development present themselves on a regular basis. It's just a case of recognising when they appear and then grasping each one accordingly. We refer to this as a learning mindset and all of the very best bartenders possess it.

> **And as with most things, the opportunities for development present themselves on a regular basis. It's just a case of recognising when they appear.**

Firstly, understand this one simple rule: you have the potential to learn from everyone. It's a mistake to believe that simply because someone has less experience than you, you in turn know everything that they know. This is a common belief and one that is mistaken. I have been training bartenders for more than thirty years. In that time, I have trained more than 50,000 people in more than twenty-five countries. It would therefore be reasonable for me to presume that I have more experience than most. In fact, many of the people I train weren't even born when I began my bartending career.

However, even though my interactions with all of these budding mixologists and bartenders are in the role of 'teacher' I find, even today, that I learn continually from them. This is because I believe in the principle that one person simply can't know everything, that each individual has something to offer and that regardless of age or experience we have different ways of working, behaving, thinking and ultimately being creative. If I didn't open my mind to the potential of what I could learn from others, I would be stuck in an era where I was a knowledgeable and skilled bartender of the time but had become subsequently out of date in terms of my views, understanding and relevance. For us all to avoid this trap we need a thirst for learning and the attitude for continual evolution.

Of course, there are also many people around us who have greater knowledge, skills and techniques than we do, and they are the most available and abundant source for self-development that we have.

The following is a list of behaviours and activities that you can put into place to drive your own development.

Learning from your colleagues

Your colleagues are the most constant and available resource for learning. We tend to work with our teams on a daily basis but don't really take the opportunity to truly watch and learn from them. This may sound obvious, but it is amazing how often we simply miss this opportunity. I often come across bartenders who are in awe of their colleagues and tell me that 'she's the best bartender here' or 'he makes the best mojito'. But while they recognise their colleague's skills, they almost never ask them to share. So watch, look, ask and more importantly, repay. There is almost certainly going to be something that you do well that you can repay them with. This is a cultural approach to working and learning and the more you do it, the more it becomes second nature and before long everyone is learning from everyone else and your standards overall are progressing.

Running your own skills sessions

Another way to learn from one another is to formalise the process. In this case, rather than simply watching and learning on the job, you arrange a regular skills session, maybe once a week, where everyone attending is tasked with sharing something. This could be a new piece of information, some product knowledge, a technique, something relating to upselling, rapport building, etc. Staging a regular session focuses everyone's mind on the learning mindset, their individual responsibility to contribute and their role in terms of mutual support and learning. It also has the knock-on effect of rolling over into service where new skills are put into practice and colleagues can support one another in that process. Additionally, it has the side effect of generating a much closer bond between the team as a whole.

Reviewing your guest interactions

One of the greatest opportunities for learning comes from every interaction you may have with a guest. In this scenario, instead of just serving someone and moving on, you take the opportunity to review your successes and failures subsequent to the interaction. In this case, I would recommend this take place after, rather than during, the shift. Simply set aside some time to think about what worked well and what didn't. Ask yourself 'why?' Why was I more successful with a particular upsell? Can you identify why you were able to influence a particular guest more effectively than usual? Did you do something different or better and can you try to repeat? Or, did things get a bit prickly with a rude guest? Was it really their fault, or did you fail to handle it properly? Were you too emotional? Did you take it personally? What could you have done differently to make the interaction go more smoothly? And, when you are next in a similar situation, will you be ready to handle it better?

This process of self-analysis has proved to be a very effective tool for those bartenders who are looking to develop their interpersonal skills. By setting aside the time to have some honest, private internal dialogue with yourself, you are much more likely to learn from your experiences rather than do what most people do, namely experience them and move on!

> **This process of self-analysis has proved to be a very effective tool for those bartenders who are looking to develop their interpersonal skills.**

Setting goals and targets based on specific techniques

All great bartenders use a particular technique to help remember a piece of new information or technique they have learned. It is called consolidation and comes from the acronym EDIC as used by many professional trainers: Explain, Demonstrate, Imitate, Consolidate. When running any bartending course a trainer will employ EDIC as a gradually more impactful method of getting the message though to their trainees.

Imagine I am teaching someone how to make a margarita. Firstly, I EXPLAIN how it is made and what I am going to do. By doing so I set the groundwork for learning about the margarita, but if I was to explain alone we would only expect fewer than 10 per cent of people to get it. The next stage is to DEMONSTRATE. In this case, by visually demonstrating how to mix the cocktail, more than 50 per cent would now get it. Having demonstrated you would now get the trainee to IMITATE you. In other words, they would make the cocktail with you looking on to provide guidance if necessary. At this stage the vast majority of people will get it. The final stage is CONSOLIDATION. This is the point at which they go solo. They mix it themselves. At this stage, the more they do it, the more it becomes permanent. And, it doesn't take long for this to happen. However, if they were to go through the ED & I stages, left the training, went back to work and then didn't mix a margarita for another week, there is a good chance that much of the learning would have been lost when the time eventually came to mix one.

Accordingly, the method Ultimate Bartenders use to consolidate anything new that they have learned is to set themselves goals throughout their shifts that pertain to what they have learned. Taking the margarita as an example, they may set the goal of mixing at least ten in the next working shift and would accordingly put in place arrangements to help them achieve this. So, for example, they may consciously look to upsell anyone ordering tequila to a margarita, they may arrange with their colleagues that anyone taking a drinks order that included a margarita pass that drink on to them, or they may arrange to have the margarita offered as a Drink of the Week, so that they had additional opportunities to consolidate their new skill. By taking this proactive, goal-setting approach to what they have learned, they ensure that anything new becomes consolidated and permanent.

Arranging distillery visits

There is nothing better for developing your knowledge of products than visiting their place of manufacture. Wineries, breweries and distilleries are simply the best places to immerse yourself in your subject matter. So why not think in terms of a bit of team-building/education? Pretty much all of these places would be delighted to host a tour of professionals from within the industry. In fact, if you were to communicate with representatives from any of the global drinks giants (the companies that represent more than 90 per cent of brands you find on bars across the globe) you would find that they would bend over backwards to accommodate you. From a personal point of view, I have done many things to develop my product knowledge over the decades, but nothing compares in terms of impact to actually going to see the stuff being made. So, pick up the phone and arrange a regular visit. Once a month, every six months or once a year. If you're not doing it you can be sure that other budding Ultimate Bartenders elsewhere are!

Joining online groups/message boards

The wealth of information available online means there is really no excuse for being light on knowledge.

Whether you want tasting notes on a whisky or a wine, instruction on how to mix a specific cocktail, technique for perfect serve, or lessons on projecting your voice or using creative language, everything is at the touch of a button. Once again, those with a learning mindset are constantly accessing this form of resource to improve their knowledge.

It is only a small minority that following long tiring shifts on the bar, are happy to dip in to their 'down time'.

The biggest barrier to this, however, is motivation. It is only a small minority that, following long tiring shifts on the bar, are happy to dip in to their 'down time' and use it to educate themselves further. A good way around this is to combine this sort of activity with the idea of running the regular skills sessions mentioned earlier. This could be one of the methods by which everyone involved in the sessions sources new information to be shared amongst the group. With a responsibility to deliver to the group on a weekly basis, you are also likely to find the motivation to go and research.

Introducing awards and incentives

Another great way to encourage learning is to introduce colleague recognition, competition and incentives. A strong way of doing this is to set up awards that everyone within your team strives to achieve. For example, it could be something like *upsell of the week, best-handled complaint,* or how about setting a goal for most positive feedback received from a guest? Once again, by introducing a scheme like this into the weekly routine you begin to introduce a culture for high performance, some healthy competition, a new dynamic to the working shift, the opportunity to be recognised and to breed a culture for learning and performing.

Buying materials (like this book)

Sounds old-fashioned, but pick up some reading material (just like you have done with this book). There are many people like myself who have made a career helping others to reach their potential. And while a live training session may come at a cost, taking advantage of our depth of knowledge and experience through a publication like this one costs less than a martini at the Rainbow Rooms!

Setting yourself daily learning/sharing goals

While we are on the subject of goal-setting... Consider setting yourself the goal of learning something new from one of your colleagues each day. By simply establishing this goal, you will positively activate the learning mindset and as a consequence will be on the lookout for learning opportunities and be more likely to find and act upon them. In a sense, it doesn't matter whether a day passes without you learning. This is more about you being in the state of mind to never miss an opportunity to do so. On the flip side, you can also set the target of trying to share some learning of your own with a colleague each day. By everyone embracing this goal-setting mindset the frequency of learning expands exponentially.

Visiting other bars (not to get drunk, to see how they do things)

There is nothing like stepping out of your comfort zone and taking a look at how other people do things. While I am fully aware that pretty much all bartenders visit other bars, most do so to relax and have a few drinks. Not enough of us recognise this as an opportunity to learn. Different bars offer their own version of great service in distinct environments, with different personalities, drinks lists and ways of working. By watching how others do things we not only have the opportunity to learn new skills but can often be inspired to find new approaches simply by seeing something that we may not have been aware of before. Throughout my early career I made it a point to visit at least one bar (on a learning visit) each week. Since then, I have visited more than 1,000 in my role as a trainer and they have continued to be an amazing source of learning and inspiration.

Stepping outside your industry to see how others do it

Also, don't make the mistake of limiting yourself to your own industry. The bar industry is about people and providing them with a great service experience. But other industries also have the same goal. Think about sales, retail, recreation, etc. If you want a great lesson on delivering guest service, you could do no better than visiting Disneyland. Or if you want to see an upselling expert in action take a trip to Harrods. Sure, visiting one of those two may not be practical for you, but the point is that there are skills being demonstrated up and down most retail high streets in shops, restaurants, even banks. You just have to find what is in front of you. With a learning mindset, you suddenly realise that you are surrounded by learning opportunities most of the time.

> **If you want a great lesson on delivering guest service, you could do no better than visiting Disneyland.**

In short, some of us will go through our lives learning at every opportunity and most of us simply won't. The difference between the Ultimate Bartender and the average bartender is that the Ultimate Bartender consistently learns from every opportunity. Some are just fortunate in that they were born with an inquisitive mind and find themselves predisposed to searching for learning opportunities. For the rest of us this doesn't come so naturally. Hence, in our quest to become an Ultimate Bartender we still have a choice. We can sit with the status quo and leave things as they have always been or we can actively work on developing a new proactive learning mindset and change the game!

TAKEAWAYS FROM THIS CHAPTER

- Never fall in to the trap of thinking that you know everything. You'll one day discover that you don't know as much as you think!

- Consider making your knowledge development a standard part of your daily routine with daily goals, and think of it as just as important as setting up or breaking down the bar.

- Take advantage of as many methods for knowledge development as possible. This will expose you to a broad range of experiences and will prevent the learning process from becoming dull.

- Remember that sharing of knowledge is also a great way of consolidating knowledge, so be generous.

- If you had to focus on a single method, there is no greater resource than the people that you work with. So, engage and be hungry to learn.

CHAPTER 3

Being Part of the A-Team: The whole is greater than the sum of the parts

This chapter looks at how the greatest bartenders leave their egos at the door while contributing to and benefiting from the power of a cohesive team.

The finest bartenders are both great team players and inspirational leaders. They view the skills of their contemporaries as strings to their own bow, understanding that with great synergy the whole is much greater than the sum of the parts. Watching a great Ultimate Bartender work within a team is like witnessing one single organic entity and here we will look at the mindset and actions employed by the very best.

. . . .

A question that often raises its head during my training sessions is this: 'What makes a great bartender?' My response is usually to throw it back at the audience and ask them what they think!

These are the most common responses:

Making good drinks

Knowledge
Confidence
Experience

However, while I agree that all four of these attributes contribute to the make-up of a great bartender, none of them rank as my number one.

The ultimate goal of the Ultimate Bartender

For me it comes down to one simple premise. As bartenders, what is our ultimate goal, our *raison d'etre*? The answer? To make our guests happy. That's it! Nothing else. Simply to make our guests happy. We are purveyors of pleasure and enjoyment and while you may think that your job is to make drinks, take money, entertain and amuse, it is in fact NOT! All of those things define your role and not your job; they are the skills and techniques that you use to achieve the goal of your job, making your guests happy. And if any of you reading this are thinking, 'Actually, my job is to make money for my boss/company/business' you are missing the point. Because if we focus on making money we tend to take our eye off the ball and do so to the detriment of our guests' experience, their happiness. However, if we are fully focused 100 per cent of the time on making our guests happy, then guess what? We tend to make more money in the process.

> We are purveyors of pleasure and enjoyment and while you may think that your job is to make drinks, take money, entertain and amuse, it is in fact NOT!

So, what indeed makes an Ultimate Bartender? People. Or rather, the greatest bartenders tend to have the best people skills. Both with their guests and their colleagues. I have met and trained tens of thousands of bartenders over the years and the relative few that I would consider to be Ultimate Bartenders all have this in common. They are great with people. Guests love being served by them, colleagues love working with them, employers love employing them. And when they move on from one job to another, people tend to follow them.

In this section, I want to concentrate primarily on the relationships that Ultimate Bartenders have with their colleagues. We will spend much time as we progress through this book focusing on the guest, but for now our focus is going to be on the team relationship. One thing that our Ultimate Bartender understands is that being part of a team is to his or hers and everyone else's benefit. He recognises that ego is a barrier to becoming the best that he could be and therefore by association realises that to become great he has to help others to also become the best they can be – and as a result will become a more skilled and rounded bartender himself.

These are the main characteristics that our Ultimate Bartender demonstrates in this regard.

Building relationships
Every truly skilled bartender also happens to be great at

developing relationships with people. In fact, you could consider bartending to be a 'people business' and as so, it's a very difficult business to excel at if people don't like you! If, for whatever reason, whether you accept responsibility for it or not, people don't like you, then becoming an Ultimate Bartender is probably beyond you. However, the good news is that getting on with people and them liking you is not just a simple matter of taste; it is more to do with what you are prepared to invest in the relationship, and with the right application and desire is a skill that can be learnt.

For example, people who embody a 'what can you do for me' attitude tend not to bond with their contemporaries as well as those who have a 'what can I do for you' attitude. And as far as our Ultimate Bartenders are concerned, this is something that helps them to develop strong working relationships with their team-mates, who then tend to bond as a result of reciprocity.

Developing a reciprocal environment (reciprocity)

Reciprocity is a social rule that says we should repay a deed in kind. In fact, it is more than a case of 'should repay' and more that we have a need to repay. For example, if you go for a drink in a bar with a friend and you buy the first round of drinks, then the social rule of reciprocity dictates that they buy the next round. This is a powerful rule, and as social beings we both adhere to it and expect others to do the same. In the above scenario, if you get to the end of the night and one of you has bought three rounds and the other just two, it is likely that the one who has bought fewer will announce that it is his or her turn to buy the first drink next time you meet. Or perhaps simply state, 'I owe you one'. This is reciprocity in action. Likewise, if the rule is broken, and your friend fails to buy his round on his turn, then we feel that he has violated the social norm, we are likely to share the information behind his back, and in time he is likely to be spurned by the social group. This is the power of reciprocity.

In simple terms, by giving generously of yourself, you create an environment where reciprocity flourishes and your colleagues essentially feel the 'need' to repay you.

In regard to the quest of becoming an Ultimate Bartender and building powerful relationships with people, leveraging the power of reciprocity within the context of positivity is an amazing tool. In simple terms, by giving generously of yourself, you create an environment where reciprocity flourishes and your colleagues essentially feel the 'need' to repay you. This repayment often takes the form of loyalty, support, friendship, etc. In other words, by giving you receive.

Most Ultimate Bartenders are the first to help others develop their skills, by sharing their own. They are the ones who step in to help when the pressure is on, who cover a shift when you are in need, who share the limelight, who put their ego to the side in favour of the team. They are interested in your opinion, recognise that everyone has something to offer and, regardless of their talent, have respect and time for you and are keen to help you become great, even if that means that you end up surpassing them. And as a result, they have strong relationships with their teams and their teams will always bend over backwards to be there for them in return. Reciprocity in action!

Building rapport

Our Ultimate Bartender is also a great rapport builder. Rapport is the sense of being in sync with someone, on the same wavelength, or of a single mind. We tend to have a natural state of rapport with the people in our lives that we are closest to. This could be members of our family, our friends or occasionally a stranger who we have just met for the first time but instantly 'clicked' with.

In the working environment, the Ultimate Bartender understands the importance of rapport in helping to develop the team dynamic and working relationship. As a result, they look for commonality: views, interests or tastes that they have in common. They are sensitive to differences in personality and so don't compete or try to impose themselves on others, but rather adjust their approach to more closely fit with the personality types of their colleagues.

This is not being 'false' or failing to be 'true to yourself' (two popular mantras), but rather being sensitive to the fact that we are not all alike. They don't take the 'this is who I am, take it or leave it' approach because they understand that many people respond negatively to that approach. Instead they work on the basis that getting on with people is to everyone's benefit, including their own, and accordingly they look for any opportunity to build rapport with their colleagues, even if the colleague concerned could be considered challenging!

As we progress through this book we are going to focus on a range of skills and techniques that will enable you to personally develop into a fully rounded, top-performing Ultimate Bartender. Your perception of what defines an Ultimate Bartender will change and broaden and you will have the opportunity to expand your skill-set into areas that you may have never considered before. All of this is designed to help you to become the best bartender you could possibly be. And yet, however good you become, wherever this journey takes you, remember that nobody has ever reached the level of Ultimate Bartender by simply focusing on themself. So, consider the importance of the above and remember that greatness lies not only in your own potential and abilities but also in your ability to be a valuable member of the team within which you work.

> **All of this is designed to help you to become the best bartender you could possibly be.**

TAKEAWAYS FROM THIS CHAPTER

- Remember the ultimate goal of your job is to make your guests happy and that everything else that you do is simply a means to facilitate that end.

- Think about what you can do to help others rather than what you can get from them.

- By fostering great working relationships with your colleagues, you create a better working environment for them and yourself and as a consequence are able, as a team, to deliver more enjoyable guest experiences.

- Accept differences in personality and look for the opportunities to develop rapport.

- Don't be an island. Be part of a stronger, supportive team that feeds the personal development of everyone in that team.

CHAPTER 4

The Amazing Benefits of 2 vs 1

In this chapter we discover why and how using two-handed serving techniques can triple your productivity.

As obvious as it sounds to use both hands when bartending, the difference between Ultimate Bartenders and the rest is what they do with their two hands. In its simplest form, the majority of bartenders will be found holding a glass in one hand while pouring a beer with the other. The top-flight bartender will conversely pour beers with both hands into two glasses that are sitting on the bar. The benefit? Faster, more efficient production of drinks while freeing up more time for the soft skills that feature in this book. There are of course countless examples, well beyond the pouring of a couple of beers, of where the two-handed technique can be employed. In this chapter, we cover these opportunities and discuss exercises that will help any bartender become a skilled two-handed operator.

....

Showing a 'tell'

In the game of poker there is a term used to describe when a player is giving away some information in relation to the strength or weakness of his hand. It is called a 'tell'. The tell can manifest itself in numerous ways. It could be something as obvious as someone blushing, a regular nervous gesture they unwittingly display when bluffing, or they may make an uncharacteristically large bet when they don't want anyone to *call* their hand. Regardless of what it is, the tell unwittingly exposes you.

In the bar industry, the biggest tell is the one-handed bartender. The one who can only pour, mix, garnish, add a straw or serve the drink with his stronger hand. The other hand plays the role of support. It will often be holding the glass that's being filled, leaning against the bar for support as the strong hand is occupied or hanging inert by the bartender's side. This tell is informing us of the lower skill level of this particular bartender. It is revealing that they have not received the benefit of a higher level of training in that they will take almost twice as long to make and serve a drink (extending to as much as three times with a large round of drinks) and that they are more likely to experience the pressure of high-service demand during a busy shift.

Employing the best example of two-handed bartending possible saves the most incredible amount of time.

I have always considered myself a bit of an expert at two-handed bartending. During my bartending career, I have twice set world records for the one-hour cocktail speed mix. This is a task where you have to mix as many cocktail as possible, one at a time, not repeating any recipe, in one hour. As you may imagine, you have to demonstrate incredible speed and efficiency to set a record at this task. Employing the best example of two-handed bartending possible saves the most incredible amount of time compared to what you may imagine it would take to make an hour's worth of cocktails. Of my two records, my second (and greater) one saw me mix 196 different cocktails, from scratch, one at a time in a single hour. That is an average of just under 18.5 seconds per cocktail!

Two compared to one

Of course, any bartender aspiring to achieve the Ultimate Bartender moniker will have become aware of the benefits of two-handed bartending, using two hands instead of one. Two hands sharing the role of constructing the drink(s), equally and with commensurate dexterity. Let's see how they compare.

If we are faced with a gin and tonic, the one-handed serve process will look something like this:

1 Lay a bev nap on the bar (if you use them)
2 Retrieve and check glass
3 Fill glass with ice
4 Add the measure of gin
5 Add the tonic
6 Garnish with wedge of lime (or lemon if you are still stuck in the 1980s)
7 Add a straw
8 Serve

This is eight separate actions, performed as such because of the restrictions dictated by using just one hand. Now let's take a look at what this would look like from a two-handed perspective:

1 Lay the bev nap on the bar with the left hand while retrieving and checking the glass with your right hand
2 Fill the glass with ice and set on the bar
3 Add the measure of gin
4 Add the tonic with your right hand while garnishing and adding the straw with your left
5 Serve

By using both hands you have reduced the process from eight separate actions to five combined ones. This probably represents a time saving of 50 per cent. Just think how many more drinks you and your team could serve throughout a busy shift if you were producing them 50 per cent faster. And this is just based on the example of making a single drink. When the two-handed technique is applied to 'rounds' of drinks, the time saving is amplified. The impact, from a productivity point of view, is profound, not to mention the knock-on effect of a satisfied guest who only has to wait half as long. In fact, from a promotional point of view for your business, fast service at busy times (Friday nights, for example) could be enough of a reason for guests deciding to return to your bar rather than a competitor's because the value of a stress-free, speedy ordering experience for your guests can't be underestimated.

Firstly, the guest experiences far more efficient service. Having the bartender produce your drinks in a timely manner is the prerequisite of a great service experience (nothing worse than watching your bartender take forever to make something that you believe you could do better yourself).

Then there is the engagement and entertainment factor. There is something wonderful about watching an artist at work. Someone who is at the top of their game with the ability to produce a drink (or drinks) with the skills and dexterity of someone who demonstrates a set of skills beyond those we would employ ourselves at home. Watching an Ultimate Bartender construct a drink with two hands, multi-tasking along the way with alternate hands pulling in different elements of the drink from different directions in a blur of creative dexterity, with your drink suddenly and imperceptibly emerging magically in front of your eyes, is something to behold and perpetuates the magical reputation of the Ultimate Bartender.

There is something wonderful about watching an artist at work.

Added to this is the benefit experienced by other guests awaiting their drink. As a guest standing in a busy bar, there is nothing more disconcerting than watching a poorly skilled, disengaged bartender toil through the process of producing other guests' drinks while you wait (no end in sight) for him to laboriously get to you. On the other hand, seeing an Ultimate Bartender in action, producing drinks with flair and style, efficiently and professionally, at break-neck speed but under control and with refined attention to detail, fills the waiting guest with confidence, a sense of positive anticipation and a reduced perception of waiting time due to the entertainment value of the waiting experience.

Finally, from the bartender's perspective: Being able to rapidly and efficiently produce rounds of complex drinks takes enormous pressure off him during busy times, aids in his ability to develop rapport with his 'audience', feeds his sense of self-confidence and changes the dynamic of his bartending experience from one of simple service to one of interactive and entertaining guest experience.

Making the transition to two hands

The key to developing your two-handed techniques lies in practice. If you have been a one-handed bartender throughout your career, then you will need to break the old habit and introduce a new way of doing things. But believe me when I tell you that the experience of moving from one to two hands is liberating, to say the least.

Consider the following...

Before we start we need to establish one of the most important rules. And that is to let go of the glass as soon as you can! OK, this may sound a bit strange, but what I mean is that you don't need to hold the glass while making a drink (like a G&T); doing so simply occupies your second hand. Instead, get used to putting the glass on the bar top, in front of the guests, and making the drinks right there, in front of them. (This is also considerably more engaging than turning your back on the guest and making the drinks on the back bar, out of sight.)

So often I see bartenders holding the glass as they walk around the bar adding the various elements of a given drink. Bringing the mountain to Mohammed, so to speak! By placing the glass on the bar top you have instantly freed up both hands. This now means, in the case of the above G&T example, having added the ice I can use both hands to pour a jigger of gin, I can start adding the tonic right-handed, while I am selecting and adding the lime wedge with my left hand (tongs of course), and as I finish pouring the tonic with my right hand and discard the bottle, my left hand is now adding the straw or stirrer. Much faster than doing each element sequentially with one hand.

Let me state right now that I realise that the demands of different bars are quite distinct. For example, if you work in a cocktail bar with an under-bar, front-facing ice chest, speed rails that hold your 'pouring' spirits and a clear bar top with few or no beer taps, then the task of making the entire drink in situ is a lot easier than a traditional pub that has ice in a bucket on the back-bar, spirits plugged into optics on the back, nothing but glassware under the bar top and

By applying these rules wherever possible, you will relieve pressure during busy periods.

often little space at all to make drinks on the bar due to the space being taken by all the beer taps. Nevertheless, whether you have the ideal environment or the most challenging, by applying these rules wherever possible, you will relieve pressure during busy periods, you'll become more productive, confident and ambitious, and furthermore, by releasing more time, you will be able to engage with your guest more effectively.

The idea is to let go of the glass as soon as you are able and don't touch it again until the drink is complete and ready to serve. A few simple tips follow to help you become more confident and skilled at using two hands.

Mixing spirits and mixers

With spirits and mixers, the first thing to change is the bar set-up. Ask yourself, how far do you have to walk to make a G&T? You should be aiming to make the drink without having to move any more than a foot or two. So, where are your most popular spirits? Are they near to the ice? What about the glasses? And the garnishes? Oh, and the mixers? If you site everything so that they are within an arm-stretch or a single step of each other then you are in a position to speed up the drink-making process and use two hands efficiently. In fact, just by identifying your top five selling spirits and mixers and then applying the above to just those five drinks, you will find that your productivity goes through the roof.

Try practising this:

- Start using your weaker hand to garnish and add straws. If you have located everything as above, you will start to overlap the elements of drink construction and your weaker hand will be active while the stronger one is pouring.

- If possible, consider pouring the spirit with one hand while pouring the mixer with the other. This has the benefit of cutting the pouring time in half while also mixing the drink more effectively during the pour.

- When constructing a round of drinks (four or more) think about how often you can have both hands pouring different ingredients into different glasses at the same time.

Mixing cocktails

As free-pouring is generally more acceptable with cocktails, we often have the opportunity to pour multiple ingredients at the same time.

- Consider pouring from both hands concurrently.

- If you have ingredients of the same quantity: Try holding both bottles in one hand and pouring simultaneously. Thus, freeing up your other hand for something else that could be a third spirit of a different quantity to the first two.

- If you use jiggers to measure: Consider placing the jigger on the bar and using two hands to pour multiple ingredients into the jigger before dispensing into the shaker or mixing glass. For example, if you are making a cocktail that requires 25ml tequila and 25ml vodka, place a 50ml jigger on the bar, take a bottle in each hand, simultaneously pour into the jigger until filled and then empty the jigger into the shaker. Compare that to doing them one at a time using a 25ml jigger in one hand and a bottle in the other and you can see the benefits. Additionally, if you get good at this technique you can take it a step further by holding multiple bottles (two's the max for most people) in each hand!

Another tip for strengthening your weaker hand is during quieter times consider making the odd drink using just that hand. While you will obviously have returned to a one-handed bartending technique, you will have done so to the benefit of the bigger picture. You will become more used to using that weaker hand to the point where it starts to become more instinctive and as a result it will start to 'look' for things to do when you return to practising your two-handed technique.

Back in the 1980s, I joined a cocktail bar where the bar manager explained this very fact to me from the outset. During the interview, he had told me, 'Everyone that works here is two-handed'. And that if I was to become part of the team I would have to dedicate myself to developing my two-handed skills. As part of his commitment to helping me achieve this he took the rather unconventional approach of getting me to work one full bar shift (it was a quiet session) with my right hand strapped to my side! I had to work the entire shift using my left hand only. Aside from the countless and obvious comments from our guests (I must have had to explain what was happening at least a hundred times), the effect was amazing. The next session, having been granted possession of my right hand once again, I found that I was instinctively using my left hand so much more. This, coupled with the constant advice and guidance I received from my manager in relation to the two-handed technique, meant that my transformation from one-handed to two-handed was almost instant. The rest, as they say, is history.

> **He took the rather unconventional approach of getting me to work one full bar shift (it was a quiet session) with my right hand strapped to my side!**

So, while I am not necessarily suggesting that you turn up to your next work shift with one hand tied to the side of your body, I am suggesting that you metaphorically do so by consciously focusing on bringing your weaker hand into play. Stick with it and persevere, even when (as you will) you find it difficult. Because, while it takes different people different lengths of time to acclimatise, the whole two-handed action will eventually start to feel natural, and you will feel the amazing benefits that become apparent as a result. This is a journey that every Ultimate Bartender has undertaken!

TAKEAWAYS FROM THIS CHAPTER

- By becoming two-handed in your bartending approach, you will mix drinks at a more productive rate, reduce time pressures, especially when busy, and project a more entertaining level of service.

- Actively focus on using your weaker hand. Within a short time, it will cease to feel counterintuitive and become instinctive.

- If you struggle to take to the two-handed technique, persevere! When you get it, it will transform your bartending experience and have been well worth the work.

- If brave enough, try my one-hand-tied-behind-back activity. It really works!

- Consider re-setting the layout of your bar to help facilitate your two-handed technique.

- Think about the most popular drinks served in your bar and rethink how you could make them using two hands.

CHAPTER 5

Upselling Guests Beyond Their Expectations

This chapter covers how possessing an opportunistic mindset and leveraging the magic of the second serve will completely transform the guest experience.

Have you ever noticed how some people are lucky in life? They always seem to be the ones who land on their feet. They are the ones who walk down the street, get stopped by a stranger selling raffle tickets, buy a few and then win the prize! Lucky, eh? What if I was to tell you that their win had nothing to do with luck but everything to do with an opportunistic mindset? In other words, the people who win these sorts of competitions have a philosophy of recognising and responding to opportunities, which means that while there is no guarantee that they will win anything, they give themselves the best chance of doing so.

....

On the flip side of this coin are the people who consider themselves unlucky. These people would never win that same competition because they live by a sceptical, mistrusting set of rules that would prevent them from ever having been in the prize draw in the first place. How many of you would simply ignore someone in the street selling raffle tickets? Indeed. And that is my point. If instead of stopping to find out what is going on, you simply blank the ticket seller, you have missed the opportunity. The opportunity of giving yourself the best chance of success. In the context of this example, the eventual winner is not really lucky; they are simply proving that the winner is 100 per cent certain to have come from the group of people taking the opportunity, whereas those who don't are 100 per cent certain not to win.

> **If instead of stopping to find out what is going on, you simply blank the ticket seller, you have missed the opportunity.**

So, what does this have to do with upselling?

It's simple really. When it comes to successful upselling on a bar, the ones who are extremely good at it are also the ones with an opportunistic mindset. They are constantly recognising opportunities to upsell and responding to those opportunities whenever they are presented.

The bar-industry advantage

So, let's establish a wonderful fact about the bar industry. Unlike almost any other retail environment, when a guest walks into your establishment they are there to spend money. In fact, they are emotionally committed to it. Within this environment upselling, when delivered as part of a tailored personal-service experience, is considered by the guest to be a higher level of service. It is not seen as being sold to. This is very different from buying a car, for example. You may buy a car from a dealership, but when the salesman tries to sell you metallic paint for another £2,500, heated seats at £1,500, reversing camera, etc., the experience is one of being sold to.

With this in mind, in the world of retail sales, we within the bar industry have a profound advantage.

The key to successful upselling is not about selling more, it is about introducing your guests to a new, improved drinking experience that they would never have found without you. The 'double-up for a pound' approach to upselling is in my opinion lazy, unskilled and has very little to do with improving the guest experience. It's a lazy way of selling more alcohol for reduced net profit and does nothing for the experience, guest rapport, reputation building and most importantly, nothing for long-term guest relations. It will, on the other hand, get people drunk faster!

It's an interesting fact that the vast majority of guests (research varies but figures of two in three have been bandied about for years) don't know what they want to drink when they walk into a bar. In fact, it's not so much that they don't know what they want as much as it is

It's an interesting fact that the vast majority of guests don't know what they want to drink when they walk into a bar.

about the fact that they are often bored with what they usually drink and when the bartender asks, 'What can I get you?', there is a short pause. As if for a fleeting moment, they are hoping for a flash of inspiration that will lead them to choose something different for a change.

We call this pause the *sound of opportunity*.

Consider these very simple examples of a guest/bartender interaction. This first one is quite typical, completely passive and reactive and misses the opportunities for upselling.

You: 'Hi, what can I get you?'

Guest: 'Ermm, oh I'll just have a vodka and Coke.'

You: 'OK, sure.'

While this example appears quite 'normal' in its interaction, it is a perfect example of a missed opportunity, the opportunity to step in and take control of the service experience, to turn a passive reactive form of service (tell me what you want and I'll serve it to you) into a proactive level of service (as you are not sure what you want, how about I make some recommendations?).

Can you spot where the opportunity lies?

No?

OK, let's look at the next example. This time the bartender has recognised that moment of indecision from the guest, the moment they pause. He has then decided to take the opportunity to offer a better service experience and a potential upsell. The key here is to respond as soon as the guest demonstrates indecision. They won't expect it and so you will also start to exceed their expectations, something that most hospitality businesses strive to achieve.

You: 'Hi, what can I get you?'

Guest: 'Ermm...'

You: 'Well, if you are not sure maybe I can recommend something for you? What do you usually like to drink?' etc, etc.

There it is. The pause, the 'ermm', the sound of opportunity. The moment that the best bartenders step in and change the service dynamic.

In this next example, the bartender has let the moment of indecision pass but has recognised a second opportunity to upsell. Instead of simply serving the drink, in this case they have started to open some dialogue about the guest's preferences. However, while this one is better than saying nothing at all, it is still missing the real opportunity for upsell and tailored guest service.

You: 'Hi, what can I get you?'

Guest: 'Ermm, oh I'll just have a vodka and Coke.'

You: 'Sure, do you have a particular favourite vodka?'

Considering the fact that the vast majority of bars will stock a selection of different vodkas (some have hundreds), the suggestion that the guest's preference wouldn't be ascertained is in itself a huge missed opportunity to deliver great service. This is so much better than simply taking the order and serving the 'house' pouring brand. It demonstrates care, attention to detail and communicates a sense of pride and professionalism insofar as wanting to serve exactly what the guest wants rather than a simple generic serve.

> **This is so much better than simply taking the order and serving the 'house' pouring brand.**

In this final example, the bartender has allowed the moment of indecision (the 'ermm') to pass but has fully taken the opportunity that followed by offering to recommend a vodka.

You: 'Hi, what can I get you?'

Guest: 'Ermm, oh I'll just have a vodka and Coke.'

You: 'Sure, do you have a preferred vodka or can I recommend one?'

The point here is that this is not in any way rocket science. This is simply seeking and responding to the opportunities that present themselves with almost every one of our guests. And if you think about the raffle ticket analogy at the start of this chapter, you will begin to understand that upselling is not about luck. It's about taking every opportunity that presents itself and acting upon those opportunities.

The average, reactive bartender will achieve very few (if any) upsells throughout a shift. The proactive bartender will achieve countless upsells throughout their shift, and in doing so will provide a proactive, tailored and engaging service experience too.

Grasping the Second Serve opportunity

During the early noughties, the UK pub and bar industry was in free fall. The economy was faltering, people had less money to spend on recreational entertainment, and as a result fewer people were choosing to spend as much time and money as they had previously in the bars, pubs and restaurants. As a result, countless pubs and bars were going out of business. In fact, at one point eight pubs a day were going in to liquidation. That's more than 2,500 pubs in a year. At that time, as you may imagine, owners and landlords alike were doing anything they could to try to attract more guests through their doors.

Popular campaigns included '2 for 1' offers on drinks, all night 'happy hours', pub quizzes, themed nights, loyalty cards, etc. The only issue with this kind of approach was that the additional cost of staging these events and offering discounts was barely covered by the additional revenue that resulted.

Around that time, I was involved with a training initiative that addressed the issue from a different perspective. The question we asked was this: instead of spending more money trying to attract additional guests, who would ultimately spend less because of the discounted offers, could we instead focus on getting the guests who were already coming in to the pubs (the ones who were still happy to pay regular, non-discounted prices) to stay for longer and have a couple more drinks than they would ordinarily?
The answer lay in a couple of opportunities. Namely, the *second serve* and, of course, the *sound of opportunity*.

The second serve is based on a simple philosophy. Can we get a guest to buy another drink after the one they have just finished? Ordinarily, we assume that if a guest wants another drink they will simply order another. However, we discovered that a well-timed proactive service approach increased the likelihood of more people having that second or third drink.

This is how it works:

Asking the question!
Imagine a guest sitting at a bar enjoying a pint of beer. If, when they have finished their drink, you were to simply clear their glass away, you are completely reliant on them having decided

that they would like another drink if you are to make another sale to them.

However, we have found that by asking, 'Would you like another?' when you clear the empty glass results in somewhere between 5 and 10 per cent more guests having another drink than would have done had the question not been asked at all. Consequently, simply by making sure that the question is asked of every single guest, you can expect an uplift of potentially 10 per cent in the sale of additional drinks.

This, however, is only the beginning!

You are completely reliant on them having decided that they would like another drink if you are to make another sale to them.

Getting the timing right

When it comes to asking the question, timing is everything. As you can see from the first stage, asking the question is about suggestion. In fact, we refer to it as suggestive selling. I suggest another drink and the guest, who may not have been considering one, now considers the offer and makes a decision accordingly. However, if we make the suggestion when the guest has already finished his drink, the chances are that their decision has already been made. The empty glass prompts them to make their own decision, and accordingly, if your suggestion comes after they have made up their own mind, it is likely to have a limited impact.

However, if you can make the suggestion before the guest has made their decision, your suggestion is likely to have a significantly greater impact. Therefore, we need to identify the point at which the decision is yet to be made but the suggestion of another drink seems appropriate. In simple terms, the perfect moment to ask the question is when there is between 20 and 30 per cent of the drink remaining in a guest's glass. At this stage, the timing of the question is appropriate (the drink is nearly finished) and the guest is more open to the idea of your suggestion as they are yet to consider the question internally.

In tests run with a variety of pubs and bars throughout our early-noughties training programme, we discovered that the uplift in the number of additional drinks sold would often be in excess of 20 per cent and in some extraordinary cases, where the entire bar and wait-staff team were fully engaged in asking the question at the perfect moment, we saw figures in excess of 30 per cent!

The key to cashing in on this opportunity is to stop being reactive (simply asking when you happen to be clearing an empty glass) and start being proactive. Namely, scanning the bar continually, being aware of where all of your guests are in terms of their drink levels and accordingly putting yourself in a position where you are able to time the question perfectly, every time. This in itself is a shift in service behaviour for many people, but the benefits are not simply about selling more. From a service experience perspective, delivering this sort of attention deals with one of the greatest anxieties experienced by guests in bars across the world. I'm referring to the moment when a guest has to stop what they are doing (eating, chatting with friends, etc.) to try to attract the attention of the bartender or waiter. This is the one experience that guests continually cite as the most irritating when trying to enjoy a social night out. And make no mistake, every second that a guest spends trying to attract attention feels like 10, every minute like 5 and so it goes on. However, by employing the working practice of 'scanning', trying to identify the perfect moment to ask the question, in one stroke you also eradicate the very anxiety that your guests would feel trying to attract attention and order another drink. In other words, their evening is never interrupted, they never find themselves with an empty glass (until they have decided it's time to leave) and as a consequence, they are more likely to stay for longer too. Big WIN all round!

> **This is the one experience that guests continually cite as the most irritating when trying to enjoy a social night out.**

Remembering the sound of opportunity

Of course, when you ask the question remain alert, as the sound of opportunity is also very likely to appear again.

You: 'I see you have nearly finished your drink, can I get you another?'

Guest: 'Ermm...'

You: 'Well, if you're not sure about another of the same, how about I recommend something else?'

Or

'Well I see that you are drinking X, you might well be interested in a Y. Most people who enjoy what you're drinking now absolutely love a glass of Y once they have tried it.'

Styles of recommendation

Once you have identified and grasped the opportunity, whether it is at the first order or second serve stage, you then have a variety of choices in terms of the type of recommendation you are going to make. The following four are the most appropriate forms of recommendation/sell in a bar.

Offering the upsell

Here the Ultimate Bartender will direct a guest to a more premium version of the product they order, normally offering them a choice of two or three products based on the style and character of the product they normally drink. For example, 'If you like the style of Balvenie, you must try one of our other Speyside malts. The Macallan Gold is delicious or if you want to stay with Balvenie, you must give the rum cask version a try, it's amazing'.

Focusing on the direct sell

Like the upsell, the direct sell is designed to introduce the guest to a more premium product and a better drinking experience. However, it differs in so much as it recommends one specific upsell product (direct) rather than offering a choice. Kind of *'if you like that you will definitely love this'*. Many Ultimate Bartenders use this technique so they can guide their guest more accurately and reduce the decision-making process to a simple yes or no rather than considering which to choose from two or three suggestions. This is often followed up at the point of service with a line like, 'Let me know how that works for you and when you come back you'll be ready to move on to my next suggestion.' This works particularly well when dealing with a large range of products from a particular product type such as whisky.

Suggesting the connected sell

Here the Ultimate Bartender will suggest something very different in style but still linked to the original drink. It could begin with, 'Sure, you'd like a vodka orange, or how about I create a vodka orange-based cocktail for you?' In taking this approach, the Ultimate Bartender is introducing the guest to a different, more flamboyant style of drink (a cocktail rather than a basic spirit and mixer) and having done so has opened the guest up to the possibility of trying drinks that combine more products and flavours, hence exposing the guest to far greater possibilities in terms of drinking experiences. For many people, stepping over

For many people, stepping over the line from a spirit and mixer to fully mixed drinks and cocktails is a defining moment.

the line from a spirit and mixer to fully mixed drinks and cocktails is a defining moment.

Recognising when to cross-sell

Within the bar environment, cross-selling is not as straightforward as within other industries. The idea is to recommend something that will accompany the first order and make it better as a result. So, for example, if you go to a burger restaurant and order a burger, they will try to sell you fries and a soft drink as additions. This is cross-selling. Within the bar setting, cross-selling opportunities are not quite so obvious but they do exist. Here are some examples:

- Bottle of water to go with alcoholic drinks.

- Suggesting different mixers to accompany standard spirits (Red Bull introduced the Jägerbomb; why not introduce your own combinations?).

- Spirit or liqueur to accompany a coffee.

- Think about food pairings too. Do you have any drinks or concoctions that would accompany and enhance the food order?

Recommendation tips

Avoiding pushy service

Remember you are ultimately trying to provide a service. Your recommendation should be motivated by trying to improve the guest experience. You should certainly not be motivated by simply trying to get the guest to spend more money. Ironically, it is those Ultimate Bartenders who are thinking about improved guest experience that actually end up getting the guest to spend more. After all, most guests are happy to pay a little more for an unexpectedly great experience.

Making the choice simple

It's all well and good displaying your range of thirty whiskies, but in terms of a guest having to make a choice, it is important to make that choice straightforward. I once witnessed a very proud bartender list off the names of sixteen gins when a guest asked him, 'What gins do you have?' Obviously, the guest was left completely perplexed by the selection. In just such a case, look to establish what sort of gin the guest is used to drinking, or whether indeed they have even drunk gin before. Something along the lines of, 'We have a really diverse range of gins here, if you can give me an idea of the sort of gin you usually drink, I can recommend a couple that you'll probably love', is likely to be a much better response; it's a much more personalised level of service, which then makes the decision completely straightforward from the guest's point of view. It also builds a level of rapport and trust between you, with the guest happy to defer to your expertise and advice.

Listening to the guest's needs

It is very easy to get carried away with your own agenda. For example, it's not unusual for a wine supplier to offer its customers (the bar and its staff) an incentive based on a particular bottle of wine. These normally take the shape of *the person who sells the most bottles of wine X over the next month will win a trip for two to our winery.* So, with this scenario in play, you find yourself with a team who are focused on selling as many bottles of wine X as possible. So, any opportunity to recommend it and they will do just that. The problem? Well, I think it's obvious. The wine gets recommended regardless of whether it is truly the best thing to recommend at the time.

Truly great Ultimate Bartenders are also very skilled listeners. They will ask the questions that get the guest to reveal as much information about their drinking preferences as possible. The premise being that the more they know, the better the choice they can make when recommending something new to a guest. So, when it matters, talk a bit less and listen a bit more.

Thinking long-term

Long-term can refer to later on in a guest's visit or can refer to the potential of a return visit at a later date. While you may attempt to recommend something new to a guest, it is not necessarily the case that they will go with it. There could be a variety of reasons for this. They may simply be very happy with what they drink. They may not be particularly adventurous and prefer to stick with what they know rather than risk trying something they may not like as much. Or they might not like the sound of what you are suggesting. For these and many other reasons, you will find that your guests will not simply follow blindly on each occasion.

However, the one technique the Ultimate Bartender does employ is the long game. Or to put it another way, he thinks long-term. With the goal being to improve the guest experience, our Ultimate Bartender understands that guests generally aren't aware of what they don't know. As a result, he is in a better position than the guests to recognise that there are other directions they can travel that will lead them to experiences beyond those with which they are familiar. In

However, the one technique the Ultimate Bartender does employ is the long game.

so doing, the Ultimate Bartender will set the groundwork, using statements such as, 'Sure no problem, if you want to give it a try later/at another time we can have a go then.' Or when they are saying farewell, the Ultimate Bartender might say something along the lines of 'Nice seeing you again, when you come by next time, I'll have something perfect for you to taste.'

By employing the long game, the Ultimate Bartender is achieving some sophisticated elements of rapport building. He is first and foremost defining the service experience as being extremely personalised and tailored to our guest. He is building a deep level of trust and rapport. He is generating a sense that the guest is a valued customer, so much so that the Ultimate

Bartender will be working on something special for him throughout his absence. And ultimately, this develops into guest loyalty and the significant likelihood that this guest will lower his barriers eventually and let the Ultimate Bartender take him on a great journey.

Showing them what they are yet to discover

It's an interesting fact that most people go through life drinking only a few different types of drink based on what they first discovered in their youth. They find something they like and are comfortable with and generally stick to that for years. But if you stop to think about that for a moment it very quickly becomes clear that it is an irrational pattern of behaviour. For example, how many drinks do you think the average bar can produce? Think about this for a second... If you have a bar with ten spirits and five mixers only, that adds up to fifty combinations to start with, based on the standard spirit and mixer pairing. If you now think of creating combinations of flavours with multiple spirits and/or mixers, you could find yourself in a position where you could offer a few hundred different drinks from that fifteen-product combination. And with most bars having significantly more products on the bar than the fifteen I have just suggested, you are then in a position where a modern bar could potentially offer many hundreds, if not thousands, of drink combinations.

Now, go back to the youth discovering the drink that he/she will drink for most of their adult life and ask yourself what chance, out of all the combinations of drinks they could have experienced, did they actually choose the one that they would like the most? The truth is that guests don't know what they don't know. And until someone takes the opportunity to point them in another direction, that is how it will stand. And this is the power of the opportunistic mindset, the thing that makes the best upsellers also the most engaging and personable service providers and the ones who attract an ever-increasing base of loyal guests to their businesses. It's because these people search for the opportunity. In fact, specifically, they listen out for the sound of opportunity.

> **The truth is that guests don't know what they don't know.**

Try it yourself. Next time you are on the bar, later today, tomorrow, whenever, listen out for it, that pause, that moment when you have the most powerful opportunity to change the dynamics of the service experience. Take control, become proactive rather than reactive and take your guest on a journey that they had never imagined they would experience when they first set foot in your bar.

TAKEAWAYS FROM THIS CHAPTER

- Actively listen out for the *sound of opportunity* and then have the confidence to step in and take control of the service experience.

- Remember that upselling is about improving the guest experience and not just getting them to spend more money.

- Consider the various methods for recommendation and make your choice based on the specific situation in any given moment (upsell, direct sell, etc.).

- Employ the second serve as a matter of course, removing any of the anxiety associated with ordering follow-up drinks experienced by guests.

- Remember that the second serve provides even greater opportunities for recommendation than the initial serve. Keep seeking the *sound of opportunity*.

CHAPTER 6

Possessing an Attitude to Serve

In this chapter we help you to gain a greater understanding of the 'ultimate goal', to focus your mindset and use that focus to underpin all your actions.

Why do we decide to work in the hospitality environment? Essentially, whether you are a bartender, a member of the wait team, front of house or a chef, the goal is about delivering an amazing service experience. This ultimate goal is often lost in the melee of doing your job and dealing with the associated challenges. However, a clear focus on the fact that everything you are doing is about delivering this unsurpassed level of service will mean that you never lose sight of what you are trying to achieve. In other words, it's not about mixing an amazing drink or making an inspired recommendation. It's about understanding that these skills are just two methods that we use to deliver on our ultimate goal. Everything is a means to an end, with that end being a happy guest.

....

So, let's pose a question that we have touched on before, 'What makes a happy guest'?

In reality, it's fairly difficult to come up with one concise coherent answer because the simple fact is that what makes one person happy will not necessarily make another happy. One of the biggest pitfalls of attempting to deliver a level of service that is designed to result in happy guests is coming up with a formula for doing so. By having one defined method, procedure or process for delivering happy guests we immediately remove the one key factor that is central to doing so. Namely, flexibility.

> **The simple fact is that what makes one person happy will not necessarily make another happy.**

The flexibility to respond to any particular guest's definition of happiness is crucial to the ultimate goal. The Ultimate Bartender needs to be able to move away from any prescribed method for delivering service in order to be able to deliver the particular version of service that any given guest would experience as having been delivered happiness.

In order to achieve this goal, the Ultimate Bartender demonstrates a flexible method of service. It's what we refer to as an attitude to serve. This is the 'what can I do to make you happy' mindset. In this instance, our Ultimate Bartender delivers a style of service that is not dictated by their own agenda but rather by the guest and their needs.

Take for example the amount of focus we have afforded to the subject of recommendation and upselling. While this style of service is, on the whole, appreciated by the majority of guests, it isn't enjoyed by everyone. The Ultimate Bartender will read this rapidly and will adjust the style of service accordingly.

Likewise, even though we consider the ability to make conversation and create rapport one of the Ultimate Bartender's strongest skills, some guests only enjoy a very fleeting moment of conversation and others don't enjoy it at all. In these cases, efficiency, speed of service and professionalism is a far more successful approach in making a happy guest than over-engaging, over-chatty 'interference'.

My 'one-trick-pony' chef

Many years ago, I employed a chef who worked in one of my bar/restaurants. He was a very charismatic guy and I thought it would be a good idea if he came out of the kitchen occasionally and briefly chatted with some of our guests. BIG MISTAKE! At first, it worked quite well. He would appear from the kitchen (in clean whites), have a quick chat with some of the guests (the ones who were open to it) and then disappear back into the kitchen. It seemed to be a successful approach. After a week or so, I noticed that he was coming out of the kitchen more frequently and, buoyed by his success, had taken it upon himself to extend the conversation from a quick word or two about the food with receptive guests to longer conversations about the food with every table. It became quickly apparent that many of the guests were starting to feel that his presence was an unwelcome intrusion. I guess the straw that broke the camel's back came when I saw him pull up a spare chair from another table and sit himself down with a couple (uninvited) to continue his dialogue!

Obviously, I put an immediate stop to his sojourns from the kitchen, but it taught me a big lesson. The first was about balance: there is a fine line between adding to the guest's experience and overstepping the mark and ultimately ruining it. In addition, it was also a reminder that what works for one guest doesn't always work for another.

You see, my chef forgot what he was there to deliver. He mistook feeling good about his new chef/maître d' role for delivering great service. He had discovered a formula and wanted to apply it to everyone. Unfortunately, he didn't possess the skills to read individual situations and adjust his role accordingly.

Just be yourself. Is this really the best advice?

For a moment, consider your personality. Are you confident and outgoing? Are you quiet and introspective? Are you a natural conversationalist? Do you like to dominate conversations? Are you happiest being the centre of attention or do you prefer to disappear into the background? One thing that I can guarantee, whatever your personality, there are those people who love you for it, others who accept it and some who consider you are 'not their sort of person'. In other words, if you are 'yourself' all the time, some people will like you and others not so much. It's just the way of the world.

Ironically, one of the statements that I often hear, especially when running training courses, is people saying to me, 'Well, that's who I am!' However, when it comes to possessing an *attitude to serve,* the Ultimate Bartender is not focused on being who he is but is more focused on delivering what the guests need in order to have a happy experience. They don't view altering their approach as being untrue to themselves but instead see it as an essential skill of becoming an Ultimate Bartender. Remember, this is work, their job and the more skills they can bring to it, the better they are at it and the more successes they enjoy. After all, they can be as true to themselves as they like in their own personal lives.

> **The Ultimate Bartender is not focused on being who he is but is more focused on delivering what the guests need in order to have a happy experience.**

Imagine if an actor announced to the director of a movie that he couldn't play the part of a particular character because 'that isn't who I am'!

By embracing an attitude to serve, the Ultimate Bartender is able to differentiate between his work self and his personal self and this altered state of mind subsequently leads to an enhanced ability to tailor himself to the situation at hand. The result is engaging in one moment, efficient in another. Entertainer for some and speedy server for others. Proactive and leading or reactive and responsive. Whatever makes the moment perfect, the Ultimate Bartender reads the guest, their attitude, body language, tone of voice, responses, and then responds in a balanced and tailored way.

Of course, if you have never considered this as a direction in which you would like to evolve your skills, then the thought of how you achieve the shift can be somewhat daunting. As with any skill, it takes time, perseverance and the making of many mistakes to perfect it. However, the biggest step along the path is always the first one and so, as long as you follow the path religiously, you will eventually get there.

Three tips to achieving an attitude to serve
Taking the first step

The very first thing you need to do is accept that in your professional role you can present numerous variations of yourself. You need to let go of the 'I am who I am' state of mind, reminding yourself that that person is 'who you are in your personal life' and that the ability to vary the version that you present to guests is one of the skills that defines and identifies the Ultimate Bartender.

Embracing failure

Next, you simply have to step out of your comfort zone and start giving it a go. Don't be afraid of failing and getting it wrong because that is the only way to get it right. In that respect, there is no such thing as failure here, it is all part of the development process. For example, if you think that a particular guest is open to some engaging conversation and a well-judged recommendation, go for it! If you remain sensitive to the way they respond and sense that they are uncomfortable, don't push it; simply accept that you misread the situation and back off to a more reactive level of service. As long as you learn from the experience you will have taken another step along the path.

Don't be afraid of failing and getting it wrong because that is the only way to get it right.

Challenging yourself

Complacency is the enemy here. The difference between the best and the rest is often a matter of perseverance. Generally, those who fail to reach the upper echelons of service delivery are not those with less talent, but those who make part of the journey, develop a few skills and then sit back contentedly, happy that they have achieved enough. But remember, the moment that you stand still, there will be someone else somewhere continuing to push themselves, repeatedly challenging themselves, moving beyond where they are now comfortable. In fact, for the Ultimate Bartender, the only comfort zone they experience is the familiarity of stepping outside of it.

TAKEAWAYS FROM THIS CHAPTER

- Be flexible in your approach. Remember that great service is not about the guest having to accept your style of service but conversely about your ability to tailor your approach to the needs of the guest.

- Remember: What makes one guest happy does not necessarily make another happy.

- Try to separate your professional and personal 'self', remembering that to achieve the goal of making all guests happy, you will need to present multiple versions of your professional self.

- Have the confidence to try something and fail. The only way to improve is by making mistakes and then learning from the experience.

- Challenge yourself to improve. Try to avoid getting to a level where you are 'content' and always look to develop further.

CHAPTER 7

Becoming a 'Heads-Up' Ultimate Bartender

This chapter introduces the power of 'heads-up' bartending and discovers how it can transform both yours and your guests' service experiences.

The biggest source of stress and anxiety for guests in a bar is feeling that they have not been noticed by the bartender (especially when it's busy). This tends to happen because the bar staff may feel under pressure, are busy making drinks and have their heads down focusing on the drinks they are mixing. In addition, avoiding eye contact with a group of frustrated guests when a bar is 'heaving' is also viewed as a method of avoiding an invitation for more stress and pressure (if I don't look at you, you can't distract me!) However, this defensive approach is in fact the catalyst for amplifying the levels of stress and disquiet and consequently, as is often the case, things can descend into a melange of hugely stressed bartenders and irritated, frustrated guests. However, as counter-intuitive as it appears, slowing things down, and lifting your head so that you have the ability to connect and communicate with your guests, acts as a powerful tension diffuser and is used by all Ultimate Bartenders to deliver amazing service under pressure. Here we discover the skills and techniques that allow you to develop your own 'heads-up' style of bartending.

....

Attendance up but heads down!

Picture this. It's a Friday evening and you are meeting with a group of friends in your local bar. The five of you arrive just as things are starting to get really busy. It is already 'five deep' at the bar, the bartenders are flying around working as fast as they can, heads down and focused on the drinks they are serving, with signals of tension and stress leaking from their facial expressions. You are standing amongst the crowd, battling with everyone to grab the bartender's attention. You have an idea of who was there before you and who arrived after, but you are already starting to feel the anxiety of not knowing whether everyone else in the crowd is as aware of their place in the 'queue' as you are. Added to that, the bartenders have gone into lock-down mode. They haven't looked at you and certainly don't know in what order to serve you or anyone else. They are feeling the pressure of the crowd's anxiety. People are leaning over the bar trying to grab their attention, others are waving money in the air or simply shouting things like *'When you're ready mate'*. None of which does anything other than feed the fire of the bartender's own stress. As a result, they lock down even further (if I don't react to you or look at you, you can't add to

> **The bartenders have gone into lock-down mode. They haven't looked at you and certainly don't know in what order to serve you or anyone else.**

my overworked stress load). In the meantime, your own stress levels have risen, other people have come into the bar after you, they have jammed themselves into the baying mass at the bar and are trying to achieve the same thing as you: to get a drink. However, you know, because the bartender is yet to acknowledge you, that he has no idea where you stand in the 'queue', and as a consequence you are not only stressing about when and whether you are going to get served, but also about whether you are going to be overlooked and someone else is going to be served out of turn before you.

This in turn now leads to the 'if that happens, what will I do?' scenario! You start to imagine the future. If he serves them first, will I say something? Will I stay quiet but angry? What if I let it pass once but he does the same thing over again? Before you know it, your own stress levels have risen exponentially and your mood has changed dramatically. At the same time, the person responsible for your disquiet, the bartender, has also been feeding his own stress levels because of a lack of understanding about the situation's dynamics and how he can alleviate the situation and everyone's stress.

Sound familiar?

It should do. This situation is repeated in bars all over the world, week in week out. Because bartenders are rarely taught about the psychology of these situations and are not armed with the right tools to deal with it. There are techniques that could enable them to turn these regular occurrences into ones that are actually positive for both themselves (the bartenders) and the guests.

We call it *heads-up* bartending.

It's not how long it takes that matters, it's how long it feels

It seems obvious to state, but regardless of how busy we are, the best way to deliver great service in a bar is to maintain communication with the guests. In fact, I would go as far as to say that the busier it gets, the more important it becomes. Even more so than getting the drinks made quickly. Let me explain: If you are making drinks quickly, but the guests are experiencing the anxieties described above, their perception of how long they are waiting is multiplied. Every minute feels like five and in the context of having not been acknowledged by the bartender, each of those perceived five minutes feels even longer with their anxiety rising by the second. If, on the other hand the bartender slows the drink-making process just a little, to give themselves enough time to connect and communicate with their guests, it has the effect of relaxing everyone, including the bartenders, and as a consequence, anxiety subsides, potentially disappearing completely, and there is no sense of having to wait very long at all. In fact, even if they do have to wait a little longer to be served, the fact that they have been kept in the loop by the bartender means that they are far more understanding than you may imagine. After all, they can see how busy it is.

The truth of the matter is, it's not that guests get irritated by having to wait longer, it is simply that, without connection and communication from the bartenders, they feel left in the dark!

The biggest barrier to achieving a heads-up technique is that when a bartender is busy, it feels counter-intuitive to him to slow down a little and give himself more time to look up. Instead, he would rather take the ostrich approach and bury his head, make the drinks as fast as he can and just hope to get through the busy period.

> **When a bartender is busy, it feels counter-intuitive to him to slow down a little and give himself more time to look up.**

From hell to heaven in one night

The best example of the positive effects of heads-up bartending that I can share is my own Road to Damascus moment that changed my approach to bartending as a young mixologist.

It was 1989 and I was working in one of London's busiest diner/cocktails bars of the time. The bar operated as a pre-dinner drinks area where guests had a few cocktails before going through to the separate restaurant area to eat. Ordinarily, a usual busy Friday evening would see a team of three bartenders and one dedicated bar-back working together. However, on the evening in question, as it was the week leading up to Christmas, to deal with the extra walk-in trade and additional group bookings, we raised the staffing levels to four bartenders and two bar-backs. So, there we were preparing for what was anticipated to be the busiest night of the year and as we got closer to opening I became aware of the fact that none of the other members of the bar team had turned up for work. A couple phoned in sick, others simply didn't turn up (in fact they never returned) and one, it transpired, had been involved in a road accident and spent the whole evening in intensive care (he recovered, in case you were wondering). The upshot of this was that on an evening where we had planned to have a team of six catering for the busiest night of the year, as the doors opened I found myself alone!

Within what seemed like seconds, people were pouring through the door like a tsunami. We were ten deep at the bar in every direction with frenzied orders being shouted from every angle. So, I dived in, mixing drinks as fast and as well as I could. Within no time at all I was feeling overwhelmed by what was going on; I could feel the tension amongst the crowd. In fact I could feel the potential of the crowd to turn into a mob! And as I did, so I decided to lock down, avoid eye contact and just work as fast as I could. In fact, I would estimate that within less than thirty minutes of the doors opening, things had descended into total mayhem, and with the negative atmosphere being highly charged, I actually started to feel scared. In fact, I remember reaching the point where I actually considered walking out and never returning. It was in one moment the very worst and then the very best moment of my career. I remember thinking, 'Why the hell am I doing this job?'

... And then it happened. Everything went quiet for me (in my mind at least), and I suddenly felt a sensation of complete peace and calm. A big smile broke across my face. It was strangely euphoric as the answer to my question dawned on me. I was doing this job because I loved it. Furthermore, I realised that the situation I was in, right there, right then, was, from a professional standpoint, what I lived for. What's the worst that can happen? Really? Within a few hours, I will have finished work and will be sitting with my friends talking about what a nightmare the shift had been. Was this really a nightmare or was I missing an opportunity to show off some of my skills and be a bit of a hero? I decided it was the latter... hero time! In that moment I was back in the room, I decided to lift my head up and do what I do best, communicate!

Communication: The hidden super-power

It was time to connect with everyone and get them on my side. So, at the top of my voice I made an announcement from behind the bar. *'Good evening everyone and a merry Christmas. As you can see, due to unforeseen circumstances, my five other colleagues haven't made it in to work tonight. So, you have got just me. But here's the deal: it will take a little longer, but I guarantee that you will all get served... and in order'.* That got a collective cheer; they were on my side and the sense of their relaxing was palpable. That single statement transformed an atmosphere of anxiety and tension to one of, 'OK, fair enough, let's give the guy a chance.'

So, I started working and talking, to everyone, to anyone, and the more I talked and mixed, the more the crowd came together, cheering me on, making jokes, laughing. The transformation was fantastic. I started putting people in queues. Not lines, but each time a new person or group arrived I would acknowledge them (still mixing drinks like crazy), tell them that it would be a while before I got to them but also tell them who they were being served after. That way they didn't have to worry about other people arriving; they simply kept an eye on the people they were being served after (who incidentally were doing the same thing). NB: This queuing system proved amazingly successful throughout my career thereafter. At one point, I even stopped and made this announcement; *'OK everyone, I'm stopping the order-taking. Instead, I will call out the name of a cocktail, just put your hands up if you want one! Ready? Long Island Iced Tea.'* Twenty hands went up, I lined up the glasses, mixed them ASAP and then handed them out with guests all mucking in, passing drinks back amongst the crowd and generally having an amazing time. Within an hour, I had taken back control. Most of the diners had been moved into the restaurant and the bar had become less crazy but equally busy.

By the time the shift was over I had learned the most important lesson about Ultimate Bartending: communication wins the day. No matter what the challenge, communicating with your guests trumps everything, whereas a lack of communication just exacerbates every possible negative scenario. And if you

I had learned the most important lesson about Ultimate Bartending: communication wins the day.

still don't get it, let me just add that although I had many occasions where guests complimented me in the bar, this was the first time that someone actually felt the need to write to my boss. When I returned from the Christmas break, the following letter was waiting for me.

Dear Sir,

I just wanted to drop you a line about a recent night out my friends and I had at your restaurant. It was our works' Christmas outing and I was dismayed upon arrival to discover that you had only one bartender to cope with the crazy number of people. We nearly walked out.

I'm glad that we didn't, though, because it was the best time any of us have ever spent in a bar. The bartender (don't know his name) was amazing. He was calm and funny, very entertaining indeed. He was making drinks as fast as he could while doing his best to keep everyone happy. It was like watching a show and the best thing was that even though we must have waited ages to actually get our drinks, it didn't seem to matter.

By the time we went to our table, we actually felt disappointed to have left the bar.

Please share our thanks with your bartender for a brilliant evening.

Yours sincerely,

Patti

PS. I hope you pay him well.

Becoming a 'heads-up' Ultimate Bartender

So, if you want to change both the guest and your personal experiences for the better, start thinking heads-up instead of down. Here are my top five tips.

Making the move

Initially, you need to get used to being able to bartend without having to constantly look at what your hands are doing. In the first instance this can be quite challenging but ultimately, the more you don't need to look at your hands, the easier it will become to look up, become aware of what is happening around you and then respond accordingly. I guess the perfect analogy is typing. When we begin to learn to type our eyes are permanently on the keys of the keyboard. However, eventually, with practice, we start to look up from the keys and just watch the words appearing on the screen. However, not everyone achieves this; for some reason, some people continue to keep their heads down, which means they are not as aware of the situation on the screen as quickly as those who are looking at it all the time. The only way to break this habit is to actively lift your head, look at the screen and eventually become more comfortable doing so. Likewise, the only way to stop focusing on your hands while bartending is to consciously stop doing so. Practice is the key!

Using eye contact

Try to use eye contact to connect with people. From a guest's point of view, lack of recognition that they have arrived is the flame that lights the fuse of anxiety and starts the whole experience rolling in the wrong direction. While you may be too busy to talk to someone who has just arrived, or you may be in the wrong place on the bar to start a conversation, a moment of eye contact and recognition (smile, nod, etc.) will do the job. It will set people at ease. They can see for themselves that you are busy, but they also feel very comfortable that you have seen them and will get to them in turn. In fact, true Ultimate Bartenders will acknowledge through eye contact and then add to the experience with one of the following:

- Eye contact plus, 'I'll just finish here and be with you shortly.'

- Eye contact plus, 'I'll just finish here and will be with you shortly. Would you like to take a look at the drinks menu in the meantime?'

- Eye contact plus, 'Hi welcome to the bar, I will be with you after this next couple here; in the meantime take a browse through our menu and see if you can find anything you like. If not, I've got some great recommendations to help you.'

Creating order out of chaos

Tell people where they are in the order of service, but do so in a positive way. Avoid stating that you are busy. If that's the case, they'll be able to see that for themselves. The fact you are not making a fuss about it will endear you to your guests even more. Guests are generally happy to wait much longer than you may think as long as they are kept informed and can see that there is a legitimate and understandable reason for the delay. In other words, if it's crazy busy, they can see that for themselves. If it's not, it may be worth explaining. Being told that they are third in line to be served is good service; they know where they are, can see when they are going to be served and will be happy to wait. Remember, if you don't tell them where they are, even if you get to them second and not third, the process of waiting, not being acknowledged or informed, will make that feel like an anxiety-filled eternity.

Guests are generally happy to wait much longer than you may think as long as they are kept informed.

Taking the positive approach

Tell them what you can do. Not what you can't do. Projecting and communicating a positive outlook, attitude and demeanour is powerfully engaging and has the impact of making the guest feel relaxed and confident in your ability to deliver. This is the difference between communicating either a positive or negative outlook. You could say, 'I'm really busy, I'm not going to be able to get to you for five minutes at least', the result of which is certain to irritate or anger your guests. Or you could say, 'Hi there, I will be with you shortly, just after these two guests, shouldn't be more than five minutes'. It is easy to see how one of these is engaging, informative and positive and the other creates ill feeling, puts up barriers and is very negative in its approach.

Prioritising the most anxious guests

Seek out the anxious faces. While you may have a system in place to communicate and engage with all of your guests, some people can slip through the net. In this case, by keeping your heads-up approach you afford yourself the benefits that come with remaining aware of what's happening with your guests. Always keep a regular scan going. Check their expressions. It's very easy to spot someone who looks uneasy or upset, etc. In doing so, take a proactive approach. Check that they are OK: have they been informed of when they are being served? Do they have any questions, etc.? These are the sorts of things that get missed constantly by a heads-down bartender. But practising the heads-up approach presents the opportunity to continually assess the current state of satisfaction with our guests and then to respond accordingly.

By utilising and perfecting the above you will eventually change the dynamics of the way you tend bar. You will suddenly experience the sensation of having more time than you imagine, even when it is very busy. It's a little like juggling three balls. When you first attempt to juggle, everything happens too quickly. You don't appear to have enough time to catch the falling balls and so you drop them. The more you practise, the better your timing becomes until eventually you can juggle with ease, with the sense that you have all the time in the world to catch and throw each ball. The experience is identical to that experienced by great Ultimate Bartenders who use the heads-up technique. While their colleagues appear under pressure, stressed and rushed, they appear to have so much more time on their hands. With the benefits of keeping your head up, allowing for all the engagement, connection, communication and rapport-building that is impossible when you are looking at your hands.

You will suddenly experience the sensation of having more time than you imagine, even when it is very busy.

TAKEAWAYS FROM THIS CHAPTER

- The primary advantage of heads-up bartending is the opportunities it provides in connecting with your guests and helping to dissipate the anxieties that they experience when disconnected from the bartenders.

- By working heads-up you will create the platform for using your improved communication skills to the benefit of your guests. An impossible task when watching your own hands!

- Make the decision to introduce a heads-up approach as your standard way of working and consider the 'typing' analogy as a method for self-motivation in the early, more challenging stages of your development.

- Once you are starting to work heads-up, start to use the opportunities for interaction by proactively connecting and communicating with your guests.

- Use eye contact, gestures (a nod or smile) or verbal interactions to ensure that you are connecting with as many of your guests as possible and laying the foundations for a level of rapport.

CHAPTER 8

Reading the Guests and Taking Control

This chapter discusses how you can extract key nuggets of information from your guests, to personalise a proactive (rather than reactive) guest experience.

Connection with our guests provides the opportunity for the gathering of information: information that can be used by the skilled bartender to provide an even more tailored, personal level of service. The more you know about the guest and their preferences, the more you are able to deliver. Here we look at a range of simple and effective techniques that can be used to build rapport, gather relevant information and then employ that information as part of a tailored service experience.

....

As we discovered in chapter 6, a truly great bartender never really relies on the guest to tell him what they want; they are always looking for the opportunity to take their guests on a journey. We have already seen how they use their opportunistic mindset to take control of the service experience and take their guests to places that they had never expected to go.

However, when it comes to full-on Ultimate Bartending, this voyage of discovery is not simply a matter of grasping the opportunity but also about reading their guests. Let's face it, no matter how good a bartender is, without some kind of guiding information it can be intensely challenging to come up with a recommendation that the guest is likely to enjoy. Of course, as covered previously, conversation and dialogue, when managed skilfully, can draw all the information you may require. But the Ultimate Bartender is already formulating a guest profile based on all the non-verbal/visual information that is available.

The following are my top invisible cues used by all Ultimate Bartenders to help deliver a truly personal guest experience.

Considering age

Think about the age of the person or people you are interacting with. A person's age not only gives us an indication of what categories of drink they may be interested in, but will also suggest motivations for drinking. For example, if you had nothing to go on but their ages, how would your suggestions differ depending upon these age groups: 18–25, 26–30, 31–50, 50 plus? While none of the information you draw from reading a guest is an exact science, and while no single consideration is going to be of definitive guidance, the more of these elements that you bring to the party, the more accurate you become in building the aforementioned profile.

So, you may have different personal ideas, based on previous experiences, about what you think fits with these age categories than other readers of this book. Nevertheless, the point that you can offer different suggestions for these age groups, based on your experience (either as a bartender or a human being), suggests that the diverse selections that you have decided upon are more likely to appeal to these age

This is a far more tailored service experience than simply treating all guests, whatever their age, generically.

groups and therefore should influence your thinking when deciding what journey to take your guests on. This is a far more tailored service experience than simply treating all guests, whatever their age, generically.

Thinking about gender

In addition to age, gender also has an impact on the direction in which a guest is more likely to want to proceed. For example, women drink more wine, cocktails and soft drinks than men. Men on the other hand drink more beer, spirits and cider than women. This doesn't mean that you are going to be correct in making these assumptions for every man or woman, but it is another indicator that can help to form your profile.

Being influenced by group size

Group size is another indicator for the Ultimate Bartender when reading their guests. Group size gives us a sense of where we should be heading from an efficiency perspective. For example, if faced with a group of ten plus and I had already made a read on their ages (mid-twenties) and their gender (female), I would probably be thinking that they would enjoy going down the cocktail route. I would now, having considered the size of the group, be thinking about cocktails that are easier for me to produce than those that would make the delivery of service painfully slow. For this reason, I would shy away from suggesting labour-intensive drinks like mojitos, old-fashioneds or Hong Kong gin fizzes and take them in the direction of drinks that are faster to produce, such as cosmos, espresso martinis or sours.

Profiling group types

When we consider the make-up of the group we have to think about the following. Are they exclusively male or female? Is it a mixture? What about the age mix? Similar or diverse? What's the apparent relationship? Friends, family, colleagues, blind date? Each potential combination of the above, added to the first three categories, now gives us a variety of guiding clues to help us take our guests along the perfect road for the Ultimate Bartender experience. For example, an all-female group in their mid-twenties is probably an opportunity to focus on wines (probably sparkling), cocktails or new spirit and mixer combinations. An all-male group of a similar age may be a chance to introduce them to that new beer you have just listed, some great whiskies or some 'challenging' cocktails like a Devil's breath! A mixed and slightly older group should re-inform your suggestions with a lean towards more premium products and a possibly higher level of sophistication in terms of quality and complexity of drink structure. Whereas a family group of mixed ages is an opportunity to demonstrate your repertoire and tailor the suggestions to take in children (a nice non-alcoholic cocktail, maybe), parents and the older generation.

Watching the clock: Time of day

This is an often-overlooked cue. But the time of day should most certainly influence your decisions. If someone wanders into the bar in the morning at 11, the offering should be appropriate for that time. Come 12.30–1 we are moving into the lunch arena and the offering should be influenced accordingly. However, at this stage we are looking for other clues. For example, do they look like they work and are on their lunch hour? If so, considering the general position of employees and employers alike, namely 'no drinking during work hours', then what you might recommend should probably be different to that which you may suggest to an older couple who are retired and not working, or for that matter people on holiday, etc. etc....

Watching the clock: Day of the week

Considering what day of the week it happens to be should also influence your suggestions. For example, a guest's state of mind or intentions regarding what they are prepared to drink can be influenced by what they are doing the following day. In this instance, during weekdays Monday to Thursday many guests will be getting up (often early) to go to work the next morning. Accordingly, what they would choose to drink may be quite different in terms of strength, volume or quantity to that which they would be prepared to try on a Friday evening when they know they have a lie-in the next morning. Likewise, while guests are often far more open to new experiences over the weekend, there is a distinct difference between their mindset on a Saturday compared to a Sunday.

The Ultimate Bartender is always sensitive to the weekly dynamics when making any kind of recommendation. It is their goal to suggest a drink that is not simply an enjoyable experience in the moment but is also one that won't leave the guest regretting their decision when the alarm clock goes off at 6am the next day.

Watching the calendar: Seasons

The time of year is also a great guide for the Ultimate Bartender when recommending new drinks. It is clear that guests respond to the seasons in numerous ways, often drinking (or trying) something specific in the summer that they would never consider during the other seasons. Pimm's No. 1 is a perfect example of this. Pimm's is considered the iconic summer punch and many millions of litres are sold and drunk throughout the summer period, with sales spiking on the hottest days. However, the truth is that Pimm's makes a fabulous long drink at any time of the year. Just think about it for a moment. Pimm's is essentially another spirit and mixer, like a G&T or a rum and cola, and yet, with the vibrant colour, fruity flavour and

> **Guests respond to the seasons in numerous ways, often drinking (or trying) something specific in the summer that they would never consider during the other seasons.**

fruit-salad garnishing (not to mention the summer-specific marketing), it is seen by the majority of Pimm's drinkers as a summer-only drink. In a way, by ordering a Pimm's the guest is celebrating the arrival of the summer months. This is similar to the mulled wine phenomenon around Christmas time. Ironically, after generations of failing to sell decent quantities of Pimm's No. 1 outside of the summer period, the company launched Pimm's Winter as the most effective method for spreading the appeal of their product throughout the year.

My point here is that we (the guest) are sensitively attuned to what we perceive as being season-appropriate in terms of our drinking choices and this is a fact that Ultimate Bartenders both understand and leverage when it comes to making the best recommendations for their guests. As a consequence, consider long refreshing recommendations in the summer; richer, deeper, more flavoursome concoctions in the autumn; warm drinks and punches go down well throughout the winter as do whiskies and other shorter styles of drink; and as spring arrives and the days start to get longer, think about introducing new creations and products just as your guests are starting to look forward to warmer months, the prospect of a holiday or the simple fact that the shortest days and longest nights are now behind them.

Naturally, living in the UK I have used the British seasons as a guide here. However, regardless of where you live in the world or what your seasons look like, a little thought about the psychological impact that your seasons have on your guests should inform your choices when it comes to recommending the perfect new drink to your guests.

Looking out for personal occasions

When your guest is celebrating a personal occasion, the potential to embellish their experience by recognising that it is a special time for them, and accordingly recommending some 'special' drinks to help them celebrate that moment, is an opportunity never missed by the Ultimate Bartender. If you stop to think about it, there are practically hundreds of occasions that a guest may be celebrating with a drink or two. Birthdays, anniversaries, births, engagements, new job, football team won the league, reunion, the list goes on. By engaging with your guests, entering into conversation – 'So what are you celebrating today?' – the Ultimate Bartender builds rapport, discovers the significance of their guests' occasion and can then deliver an amazing tailored experience by recommending some great new 'celebratory' drinks that will make their experience an unforgettable one. It is fair to add that on the whole guests are probably more open to drink recommendations when they are celebrating a special event or occasion than at any other time.

Celebrating universal occasions

Of course, occasions are not only limited to the guests' personal circumstances. In addition, there are those universal occasions that we all share. When, for a few fleeting moments throughout the year, the sense of celebration is enjoyed by us all and leads us to being more sociable and friendly than is generally the case and as a result, as with the personal occasions above, the guest is more open-minded and adventurous, and therefore more likely to go with your recommendation than they would at other times of the year. The obvious one is Christmas; however, there are many others.

For example, St Patrick's Day. Guinness has really made this a massive day for sales. However, the Ultimate Bartender sees it as an opportunity to introduce his guests to a range of other Irish-themed drinks, whether it's the perfect moment to introduce the Scotch whisky drinker to a nice Irish one or to promote some other Irish-related products in the form of a different spirit and mixer combination or a cocktail. Whether it's Easter, the Queen's Jubilee, the Olympics, the Champion's League, New Year's Eve, or any other of the plethora of universal occasions, the Ultimate Bartender works hard to recognise the opportunity to recommend some amazing drinking experiences to his guests at the point at which they are most open to trying them.

Observing a guest's dress style

Finally, notwithstanding any of the above, a guest's style of dress can often give a great clue as to their state of mind and intention when they enter a bar. Formal, casual, party dress, scruffy, etc., each style provides the Ultimate Bartender with a starting point, something they can build upon to profile their guest and set off along the path of transforming the service experience, tailoring their drink recommendations and introducing the guest to the world of possibilities that lie tantalisingly beyond that which they would normally drink.

As you can see from the above, while reading the guest is by no means a precise science, the more clues and indicators you draw on the more accurate your profile build is likely to be. Add to this your ever-improving experiences and in time you're are likely to become highly skilled and impressively accurate in making your 'read'. As with everything I am covering in this book, it comes down to practice. The more you challenge yourself to read your guests the better you will become at it. In terms of the opportunity for practice, it is always there. Every guest who walks through your door presents you with an opportunity to practise and test your reading skills. So why not take that opportunity?

> **Every guest who walks through your door presents you with an opportunity to practise and test your reading skills.**

Make it fun too. Set yourself the task of reading your guests and then discovering how accurate you are. You will find that on occasions you will nail it perfectly and yet on many others you will be way off the mark. However, it is by making inaccurate 'reads' that you will provide yourself with further opportunities to learn from your mistakes, which in turn will help to build your reading experiences to the point where you will eventually have tried and failed so often that your experience level becomes massive and your reading skills become very accurate indeed. At this point you will have reached the level demonstrated by all Ultimate Bartenders.

TAKEAWAYS FROM THIS CHAPTER

- Remember that your guests will provide you with a huge amount of non-verbal information and you can use this to provide a uniquely tailored service experience. You just have to look in the right places.

- Age, gender, group size and mix will all point you in the direction of potential personal preferences.

- The time of day, week or year should guide you in terms of style of drink serve.

- Key dates in the yearly calendar (Christmas, Easter) plus one-off occasions (football World Cup, Queen's Jubilee) should also guide you in terms of the mood of your guests.

- Dress code will provide clues to the nature of your guests' visit, be it relaxed, celebratory, formal, etc. Accordingly, you can use this information to make recommendations that are appropriate to their occasion.

CHAPTER 9

Living the Mantra, Knowledge is Bartending Power

This chapter covers some simple techniques for developing great product knowledge and leveraging its impact.

Here I want to build a little further on the areas that I introduced back in chapter 2, mainly because the subject of deep knowledge is fundamental to the delivery of many of the topics we have now covered. Remember, Ultimate Bartenders always back up their social and interactive skills with a deep knowledge base. This product knowledge allows them to guide, recommend and support guests through new and exciting experiences.

··············

As I have previously mentioned, Ultimate Bartenders don't simply wait for learning opportunities to be presented to them. They have a number of techniques that allow them to consistently build their bank of knowledge in regular, easy-to-assimilate, bite-sized chunks. Learning becomes instinctive and fluid without requiring profound periods of study and focus. By using a selection of visualisation and experiential techniques, followed by an integrative approach to their bartending activities, Ultimate Bartenders are able to develop their knowledge at a staggering rate without ever feeling the burden of having to rely solely on formal, dedicated training sessions.

Firstly, allow me to reiterate the point about the availability of brand-sponsored training sessions. In pretty much all cases, it is in the interest of the alcohol producers and major parent companies that any person working in Food & Beverage within any form of hospitality business has a strong knowledge of their products. To this end, whether we are talking about wine, beer, spirits, mixers, soft drinks or hot beverages, the brands tend to have their own experts/trainers available to run dedicated training sessions on their products. If you would like a particular company to run a training session for your staff, all it generally takes is a call to that company and they'll arrange a session for you. In addition to the general sessions, the big drinks giants, companies like Diageo, Bacardi Brown-Forman, etc. also have much bigger, centrally run training facilities such as Diageo's Bar Academy and Bacardi's Legacy Initiative. These are dedicated, industry-focused training 'organisations' that exist within the structure of the parent companies that individuals or businesses can join directly to access their full range of training aides, including videos, blogs by industry experts, live masterclasses, competitions, etc.

Taking responsibility for your own development

Once you have made the most of the brand-sponsored training opportunities, it is advisable to think in terms of taking responsibility for your own ongoing development. Because, when you consider the thousands of products available and the depth of knowledge it is possible to achieve with each product, you could spend a lifetime dedicated to becoming an expert on everything a bar could offer and still not get anywhere near that level. I refer you to my whisky/*Mastermind* experience as described in chapter 2.

> **When you consider the thousands of products available and the depth of knowledge it is possible to achieve with each product, you could spend a lifetime dedicated to becoming an expert.**

In truth, the development of knowledge in most subjects tends to be more effective if it is done in regular bite-sized pieces and in an experiential way. Take this book as an example. If you were to read it from cover to cover in one hit and then walk away from it in the hope that you are now an expert in all the areas I have covered, you are likely to be disappointed. However, if you were to take each skill area in isolation, read it, put it into practice, come back to the book again as a method of refreshing the techniques and ideas, practise more, learn from your mistakes, etc., you are far more likely to become highly skilled in all of the areas we cover and as a result reach the Ultimate Bartender level. Within this learning context, while brand-sponsored sessions have their role, they alone will not get you to the level of knowledge that the Ultimate Bartender would desire. Instead, think of the brand sessions as a supplement to your own development programme.

One of the methods I teach for self-development, which takes in the bite-sized experiential approach, and I touched upon in chapter 2, is as follows. Let's imagine that you stock twelve different gins on your bar. The very fact that you are offering such a wide selection suggests that each one has a distinct variation in style, flavour and character to the others. It suggests that the drinking experience of each should be unique. Of course, they should all be recognisably gin, but they should all be different. If not, why bother having them? And, from the guests' perspective, outside of the gins that they are used to drinking, they probably don't know the differences at all. In fact, most guests who choose a specific gin don't necessarily do so because it's their favourite one; it's often because they tried it at some point, liked it and consequently stuck with it. In some cases, the gin they have chosen was based simply on the branding and marketing that surrounded it. The only chance that they will try a different gin is if someone (the bartender) recommends one.

And yet, when it comes to recommendation (as we discovered earlier in this book), simply suggesting to a guest that they should try something else is often not enough. They want to know why? What's the difference? What does the one you have suggested taste like? Why will I prefer it to my usual choice? And this is where the vast majority of bartenders are exposed. With limited knowledge of the products, a bartender can quickly become unstuck, rendering their attempts to recommend unconvincing and the likelihood that a guest will follow their suggestion non-existent. To operate in the upper echelons of the

Ultimate Bartender you will need to have a level of knowledge that will enable you to speak with confidence and authority about any product or drink you may recommend.

All it takes is ten minutes a week

Back to the twelve gins. Firstly, set yourself the task of arranging a regular, weekly, ten-minute 'buzz-session' with your bar colleagues. This could be an independent meeting, either prior to or subsequent to one of the weekly bar shifts. Alternatively, it could be inserted into any regular briefing session that takes place. Start by selecting two of the twelve gins that you stock (it's good to go with your house/pouring brand plus one upsell) and assign the role of buzz-session leader to a member of the bar team (it's a good idea to run the first one yourself). Over the coming week, leading up to your buzz-session, it is the leader's responsibility to research some information about each of the gins you have chosen. This could be distilling method, botanicals used, history of the product, USPs and, most importantly, some tasting notes. When the buzz-session arrives, it is the leader's job to run a brief impactful session sharing some key nuggets of information about each gin (I would keep it to no more than three pieces of information to start with), allowing every member to have a taste of the gins in question, to share the tasting notes and also discuss the team's own opinions in terms of flavour and preferences. If you have time, you can also cover the topic of versatility and

> **The key here is to keep the session short and impactful; you don't want to overload anybody's brain.**

mixability. The key here is to keep the session short and impactful; you don't want to overload anybody's brain, just share some easy to remember points, while giving the team their own experience of tasting and discussing the products. Following the buzz-session, it is every team member's goal in the coming week to take every opportunity to share that information with a guest where it is relevant to the guest's experience (see Chapter 2: Setting goals and targets based on specific techniques). In doing so, those small pieces of information will become inexorably etched on the memory of the bartender and they will be able to talk confidently about it thereafter. In the meantime, each week the buzz-session leader will select another member of the team to become leader for the following week and likewise selects another one of the ten remaining gins for them to cover in the next session.

By continuing this practice on a weekly basis, you can keep the sessions short and it becomes easy to remember the experience and information, and to engage in the practice of actively using that information over the coming week to enhance the guest's experience. Furthermore, the process of every member taking responsibility for their part in the full bar-team's development means that within eleven weeks everyone on the bar team will be able to speak confidently about every gin. Once the gins are covered, move on to whisky or vodka, until your spirits are covered. Thereafter, cover your beers, wines, softs, cocktails, etc.

In just one year, you could find yourself in the position where you could speak confidently about fifty-two products. For some bars this more than covers their whole stock range. For others, it barely scratches the surface. However, what is clear is that there is a huge number of bartenders who know very little about the products that they sell. And yet, by taking this simple approach to your personal product-knowledge development, the speed at which you will become more knowledgeable than the majority of bartenders is rapid. And, if you stick with it, it won't be long before you are one of the most knowledgeable bartenders out there... just like our Ultimate Bartender.

As a final thought, ask yourself how many weeks have you been bartending for? If it's three years, that's 156 weeks. Now, ask yourself how many products could you speak confidently about to the point that you could describe their taste, how they differ from similar products, how and where they are made, what their history is? Is it 156? If not, then that's a missed opportunity. Five years, 260 weeks, 260 products? No? OK, you now know what to do about it.

Visiting the producers

I referred earlier to the power of experiential learning. This is when actually experiencing something has a far more dramatic effect on your ability to remember it than simply reading about the subject or listening to someone speak. Running a tasting session for example, when you actually get to taste a product, is far more likely to leave you in a position where you can speak confidently about that product's flavour profile (from experience) than if you had simply tried to consign someone else's tasting notes to memory.

I would therefore once again recommend, as part of your knowledge development, exposing yourself to as many experiences as possible. Remember, there are development techniques that benefit from group participation, such as the group tasting sessions mentioned above. However, there are also many opportunities for development that you participate in alone. Think of books, videos, lectures and training sessions as valuable resources for your development, but if you want to become a truly knowledgeable Ultimate Bartender, don't rely on them alone. I have mentioned this before, but one of the greatest learning experiences I can recommend is to visit the places where the products are produced. There is nothing quite like walking around a distillery, vineyard, brewery or soft drinks factory, in the company of the people who actually make the stuff, to get a true understanding of the processes.

From personal experience, as a young enthusiastic Ultimate Bartender in the making, I read extensively on the production of spirits and the diverse methods of distilling. My knowledge was fairly reasonable. However, once I started to visit distilleries and witness the processes first-hand, my knowledge and understanding went through the roof. In fact, I would suggest that a couple of hours spent in a distillery with an engaging guide will provide you with a depth of knowledge (certainly in relation to the specific product produced at that site) far beyond that which you could get from books alone.

Becoming a bit geeky!

Another tip I would offer to aid in the development of your knowledge is to spend time with like-minded people getting geeky. In my earlier years in particular, I learned more about cocktails outside work than I did during my shifts. By mixing with other cocktail mixologists, sharing experiences and getting geeky about cocktails, mixology, spirits, etc., I discovered far more than having simply gone through the formulaic training that all new mixologists were compelled to experience. Mixologists like to 'show off' their knowledge to one another; we enjoy demonstrating our skills, discussing stories, coming up with variations (often getting drunk in the process). As a result, if you are open-minded and hungry for new information, your colleagues and the wider mixologist/bartender community can be the greatest source of all.

Spend time with like-minded people getting geeky.

Whatever you do in your quest to become an Ultimate Bartender, the key to success lies in your desire to continue improving. Whether we are referring to physical skills, communication techniques, or as we have discussed in this chapter, your general subject knowledge, it is your hunger and desire to develop that will define the level you achieve. As I have mentioned on many occasions in this book, as with most things in life, the opportunities are there for everyone; you either see them or you don't. Many years ago I ran a training session for the staff of a local community pub. Approximately twelve people attended the session, of average age twenty to twenty-five. That was all except one gentleman named George, who had worked in that pub for an impressive forty-two years! I was warned in advance that George was pretty well stuck in his ways, that he had seen and done it all and that he had a 'you can't teach me anything' attitude.

Been there, seen it, done very little!

As the session got underway, it became clear that the warning I had been given about George was indeed correct. He knew it all (or at least he thought he did). In reality, what George knew was very little. He knew how to serve a drink 1970s style, how to take an order and how to take money. All perfect for running a bar in the 1970s. But by the standards of a modern multi-skilled Ultimate Bartender, his knowledge and skill base was limited at best. What was most striking for me was how little he knew about the products he served. He had absolutely no idea how they were made, what the differences were, their relative alcohol content or the base ingredients. He didn't even understand the difference between a fermented product such as beer or wine and a distilled product like a spirit. He even proudly told me that the only difference between whisky and brandy was where they were made. Outside of that they were identical!

> **What was most striking for me was how little he knew about the products he served.**

For me, George was an example of someone who had missed countless opportunities. He had been taught the basics of how to serve a few drinks back in the 1970s, had found that was enough within the context of the place he worked and had continued to do the same thing for the next forty years or so. But just think about the opportunities that George had let pass him by. Had he done no more than engage in the buzz-session activity that I described above, after his forty-two years, or 2,184 weeks, his depth of knowledge would have been outstanding.

So, I urge you, if you are sincere about wanting to become an Ultimate Bartender, focus on your knowledge development. It will enhance many of the other skill sets that we have covered in this book. It will set you apart from the vast majority of bartenders working in our industry and it will enable you to deliver service experiences that mark you out as one of the best in your trade.

Don't be a George!

TAKEAWAYS FROM THIS CHAPTER

- Remember that a broad depth of knowledge will help to underpin all attempts to recommend, and therefore you should actively look to develop it. A day without learning something new is simply a missed opportunity.

- Learn using the experiential 'bite-sized' model and look to consolidate your learning by taking all opportunities to share your knowledge when it is new to you.

- Encourage group learning amongst your colleagues and share the responsibility for developing your buzz-sessions.

- Think outside of simply learning on the job and look at the opportunities for learning that exist outside your place of work. For example, a distillery visit.

- Get geeky!

CHAPTER 10

Connecting with Guests and Influencing their Decisions

In this chapter, we focus on the importance of great communication skills. Here I will share how to develop and harness improved body-language skills, leverage reciprocity, use expressive and creative language, and project passion and enthusiasm to ultimately deliver an inclusive service experience.

Ultimate Bartenders have a way of 'selling' new experiences to us in an emotive and engaging way. By using creative language to 'sell the sizzle', and projecting passion with positive body language and expressive use of voice, they tend to have most guests eating out of their hands. And this is precisely what the guest needs in order to open them up to unforeseen experiences that exceed all their expectations. Here we share a range of exercises that can help any bartender to discover the creative communicator within and develop those communication skills within the setting of their working environment.

....

When we talk about influencing techniques it's easy to assume that there is something a little cynical or even immoral about using a technique to influence a guest's decision-making process. However, although there are many so called 'skills' that can be leveraged by and to the benefit of unscrupulous sales people, in the context of becoming an Ultimate Bartender, they are techniques that we use to enhance the guest experience and hopefully help nudge our guests in directions that they would ordinarily miss and which are ultimately to their benefit.

Selling the sizzle

At any stage that we decide to recommend a product or drink type to a guest we are in fact trying to sell them on the idea. In this case, relying solely on what we say (the facts) is not necessarily enough to do the job. Essentially, we are trying to create a response, in the way advertisers do when they hook us in on a new product. They focus on using creative, emotive language and, in the case of TV ads, combine them with expressive vocal delivery. The resultant effect is referred to as 'Selling the Sizzle' and comes from the slightly longer phrase, 'Sell the Sizzle, not the Sausage'. In simple terms the phrase refers to using language and voice to create the same emotive responses that you would get from standing watching a sausage cooking on a barbecue. In other words, your language and delivery take the place of the sight, sounds (the sizzle) and aromas released by the sausage.

Essentially, we are trying to create a response, in the way advertisers do when they hook us in on a new product.

The whole idea is to elicit an emotional rather than reasoned response. If I was to tell you that I'm selling a sausage that is 97 per cent pork, contains no additives, has a range of herbs and spices and is gluten-free, you would consider the facts and make your reasoned decision based on them. On the other hand, if I was to stand you next to me while I cooked that sausage on the barbecue and you could see it browning, hear the gentle sizzle and smell the gorgeous aroma, your decision as to whether you wanted one would have nothing to do with the facts; it would simply be an emotional response to the wonderful sensory reaction you are having.

Accordingly, by using creative language and expressive vocal delivery we are trying to achieve the same thing: to avoid a reasoned, considered response based on facts and draw out an emotional one based on perceived experiences. In other words, a whisky described as a single malt, aged for twelve years in oak barrels and bottled in 2004 is likely to get a reasoned response based on those facts. However, the same whisky described as a soft and smooth single malt with warming undertones of caramel and a deep, rich and luscious chocolate finish will get an emotional response based on how 'yummy' it sounded.

Understanding the role of the limbic system

The limbic system is a complex region of the brain that takes in the hypothalamus, the hippocampus, the amygdala and several other nearby areas. It is primarily responsible for our emotional life and plays a significant role in the formulation of memories. The limbic system also plays a major role in our decision-making process, in particular when that decision is an emotional one. For example, when choosing to purchase something pleasurable, like a whisky. However, it is worth understanding that because, in evolutionary terms, the limbic system is very old and pre-dates the development of human language, as a consequence it still has no capacity for language. Or in more basic terms, it doesn't comprehend words. Instead, it responds to emotions. Accordingly, if when trying to recommend a glass of whisky we concentrate on 'selling' the facts (example above), the limbic system won't respond and therefore won't become involved in influencing our decisions. However, as soon as we speak in emotive, descriptive terms, the limbic system begins to respond emotionally and consequently begins to influence our decision-making process.

If you have ever looked at something like a beautiful Ferrari, a Rolex watch or a designer handbag and experienced a feeling of desire ('I really want one of those'), what you are actually experiencing is the impact of the limbic system. Your response is not rational, you don't need the item, it is probably ridiculously expensive for most of us, and yet, in the pit of your stomach, for a fleeting minute or two, you wish you owned it, because you imagine how great it would *feel*.

Once we understand that simple fact, it gives

> **If you have ever looked at something like a beautiful Ferrari, and experienced a feeling of desire ('I really want one of those'), what you are actually experiencing is the impact of the limbic system.**

us a profound advantage when we are endeavouring to convince a guest of the wisdom of following our recommendation. By describing the experience of imbibing your suggested drink, you are likely to be far more successful in terms of uptake when recommending new drinking experiences.

So, as you can see, when it comes to communicating verbally, the combination of expressive vocal delivery and creative, descriptive language combines to create a powerful emotive image, one that is experiential for the listener and more likely to result in a positive emotive response.

Albert Mehrabian's communication model

I have always believed that our sophisticated ability to communicate is what defines us (humans) as the dominant species on the planet. We are by no means the physically strongest but we are by far the most intelligent, and an ability to communicate complex ideas, emotions and information has resulted in us building the world in which we now live. Likewise, it is also my belief that the strongest communicators amongst us tend to rise to the top. Whether it is in business, entertainment or politics, and whether it is for good or bad, the most charismatic and engaging communicators seem to be the ones who succeed in their goals to the highest level. As humans, we thrive on connection. Our need to interact with one another, to express our beliefs, feelings and opinions is what makes us who we are. Therefore, it is no surprise that the better we are at communicating with a broad range of people the better we become in terms of achievement. Consider the following historical characters: JFK, Henry Ford, Nelson Mandela, Steve Jobs, Martin Luther King... they didn't reach the amazing heights they achieved by coincidence. What they all had in common was passion, a goal, drive, charisma and a unique ability to communicate that to the largest audience possible, an audience that in turn felt what these leaders believed and accordingly bought into the visions they shared.

It therefore makes complete sense that the most successful people within the hospitality industry are also the ones who can communicate their passion, enthusiasm and charisma to the broadest audience.

We have already looked at the effect that creative language and expressive vocal delivery can have on a guest when communicating an idea or suggestion, but to fully understand the complete set of communication skills, I need to introduce you to a gentleman by the name of Albert Mehrabian.

Albert Mehrabian was born in 1939 in Iran and at the time of writing is currently Professor Emeritus of Psychology at UCLA in California. He is best known for his publications on the relative importance of verbal and non-verbal communication, the conflict that can occur between the two and for introducing the '7%-38%-55%' rule.

It's not what you say, it's the way that you say it (and project it)

The above rule refers to the relative impact of the three main elements of productive communication. Productive communication refers to communicating outwardly, when you are the one speaking. When you are on the receiving end of communication, for example listening, it is referred to as receptive communication. The rule breaks down as follows:

7 per cent is *words*. These are the words that make up our languages. At first sight, especially if you haven't heard this before, 7 per cent appears to be a very low number when you consider how sophisticated and evolved our languages are. After all, pick up a dictionary and you'll find many tens of thousands of words in there. However, words alone can be misleading and are often misunderstood in terms of meaning and inference. Consider for example how easy it is to misread the tone, meaning or intention of a text message! This is because, to truly give our words clear meaning and context, we need to add something else. Our voice!

38 per cent is *voice*: Generally speaking, when we consider our voices there are three elements that come into play. These are tone, pace and volume. Our ability to regulate all three provides the missing link for words alone, as described above. And yet if our voice doesn't match the intention of the words it can create confusion in communicating the message, as shown in the following example.

Words: 'I really like your hat'

Voice: Sarcastic, irritable, frustrated

So, do I really like your hat or am I trying to insult you? Well, with the voice being a much stronger communicator than the words, the voice would win out here. If you were on the receiving end of this statement you would absolutely feel that I was insulting you. But what if the issue with my voice had nothing to do with your hat but instead was as a result of something that happened to me in the moment before I made the statement? Maybe I had just come out of an argument with someone and I was still feeling its effects, maybe I'd had a bad day, was bored, feeling miserable, etc. The fact is that on many occasions, if we fail to realise the impact that events or emotions can have on our voice we can easily communicate a message different from the one we had intended.

> **If you were on the receiving end of this statement you would absolutely feel that I was insulting you.**

Another example of how our voices can sabotage the intention of a message is when we emphasise the wrong word. In these cases we can actually change the entire meaning of what we were trying to communicate. Take the sentence, 'I didn't steal the hat' and consider the following three versions, vocally emphasising the underlined word.

'I didn't steal the hat'

By emphasising the word 'I', the suggestion is that someone else stole the hat.

'I didn't <u>steal</u> the hat'

By emphasising the word 'steal', the suggestion is that I have the hat but I just borrowed it.

'I didn't steal the <u>hat</u>'

By emphasising the word 'hat', the suggestion is that I did steal something; it just wasn't the hat.

In these examples of a simple five-word sentence, you can see how vital the role of the voice is in communicating a clear message and how easy it could be to communicate a completely incorrect one, even though the words remain the same. Now imagine how easy it is to miscommunicate a message with the thousands of words we speak every day and it becomes clear how fragile the relationship is between the two (words and voice). And yet, when it comes to the most effective communicators we witness a consistent behaviour, the idea that how we say something is far more important than what we say.

> **In these examples of a simple five-word sentence, you can see how vital the role of the voice is in communicating a clear message.**

And yet, even when we combine our words and our voice, as far as Albert Mehrabian is concerned, we still haven't considered the most impactful element of communication.

Body talk

The third part of the rule, 55 per cent, is *body language*. Body language is the big non-verbal communicator and it has a more profound impact on the receiver than words and voice combined. In addition, what we communicate through our body language is not necessarily congruent with what we are saying, but conversely tends to reflect what we are thinking or feeling. As a consequence, if we are verbally communicating a statement but feel quite different internally, our body language is likely to communicate that discrepancy and as a consequence leave the receiver with a sense of conflict. And on the whole, because body language is a more impactful communicator, it tends to dominate the sense of what the receiver perceives. If you have ever had someone tell you 'I'm absolutely fine' and yet you know, because their body language is communicating something to the contrary, that they are anything but fine, then you will identify that you have experienced this. Now consider the following example.

Verbal: 'I have no problem with you'

Non-verbal: No eye contact, looking down, arms crossed

In this example, it is most likely the receiver will trust the predominant form of communication and trust their 'feeling' that the speaker does indeed have a problem.

Avoiding communication conflict

So, to become a more effective productive (outward) communicator our goal is to try to avoid conflict between the three communication elements while making them work in perfect harmony. The perfect scenario being the combination of more frequent use of creative language, together with complementary expressive vocal delivery that expresses the intention of your statements tonally, and finally, to be delivered with supporting, non-conflicting body language.

Of course, this is easier said than done because the conflicts that occur are also the very things that make us human. However, by considering these three communication elements as skills rather than something that we just do, we are able to focus on their development in the same way we would if we were to try to improve any other skill. In fact, it is because we tend to accept that the way we communicate is just that – the way we communicate – that it doesn't occur to us to work on developing it.

However, another natural ability we all have (assuming that you are fortunate enough to be able-bodied) is that to some extent we can all run. However, if you wanted to become a better runner you would start to train, develop your technique, improve your fitness and ultimately become a better runner than you currently are. Likewise with communication. No matter how good you naturally are at it, by stretching yourself, challenging your perceptions of how you currently communicate, expanding your understanding of how things work, focusing on developing your vocabulary and putting it to good use, 'listening' to the sound of your vocal delivery and then trying to develop it further, and finally considering your body language, questioning your stances, facial expression and gestures, you will, as in the case of running, begin to improve and become the more impactful communicator that is within you.

Perfectly communicating a recommendation

Now let's take the example of recommending a whisky that I referred to earlier in this chapter. You may remember that we already made the most of the function of the guest's limbic system by avoiding the factual description of a single malt as 'aged for twelve years in oak barrels and bottled in 2004', and instead went for the more emotive description of a 'soft and smooth single malt with warming undertones of caramel and a deep, rich and luscious chocolate finish'. Here we are already maximising the impact of 7 per cent of Albert Mehrabian's model.

Now imagine this being delivered in the perfect tone of voice, one that communicates the speaker's passion, his personal love for the whisky, his enthusiasm in having the opportunity to share the information with you, his sense of how delicious the flavour characteristics are and his confidence in how much you are going to enjoy the experience. Indeed, imagine it being spoken in the tone of an M&S food advertisement and you start to understand how the voice can profoundly enhance the experience of the receiver. Done well, the guest's limbic system would be in overdrive, and they would be almost powerless to resist. This is in stark contrast to it being delivered in a 'matter of fact' tone, as if it was the thousandth time you had said it, or as if you were reading it from a script. Making it sound fresh and desirable is now drawing on the next 38 per cent of Mehrabian's model.

And finally, if all this is accompanied by complementary body language cues such as positive facial expressions, sensitive hand gestures, strong use of regular eye contact and a general open, confident and relaxed stance, you will have hit the communication jackpot, by leveraging Mehrabian's final 55 per cent and becoming a 100 per cent communicator.

Be aware that the journey to communication greatness is a continual steady progression. It won't be an overnight transformation in terms of results but will require an overnight shift in your desire to develop. As with other areas of skill development in this book, the biggest step is first to recognise the opportunity for development, then to make the decision to do something about it, and then commit to the long-term ongoing quest to become the

The biggest step is first to recognise the opportunity for development, then to make the decision to do something about it.

Ultimate Bartender you know is within you.

Of course, great communication is not simply about recommending a drink or two. It impacts every aspect of your life whether it is at work with your guests and colleagues or with your friends and family. Every moment that you find yourself in an interaction with another human being is an opportunity to develop your abilities and put your improving skills to work. Relationships will improve, happiness evolves (for you and those you come into contact with) and you start to perceive and experience both your personal and working life from a fresh enhanced perspective.

Using reciprocity as a tool for great service

At the beginning of this book, I referred to the concept of reciprocity as a tool for helping build relationships between colleagues. I am returning to the concept of reciprocity once more as it could also be considered an influencing technique when used as part of the service experience and work to the ultimate benefit of the guest. When used correctly and communicated effectively, reciprocity is an incredibly powerful influencing technique and one used by all of our Ultimate Bartenders.

To reiterate, reciprocity in social psychology refers to responding to a positive action with another positive action... rewarding kind actions. As a social construct, reciprocity means that in response to friendly actions, people are frequently much nicer and much more cooperative than predicted by the self-interest model, in which we are more likely to put our own interests and agendas first. In simple language, we all experience the social need to repay a kind or generous deed. If someone buys you a drink, you will want to buy the next one (reciprocity in action).

So powerful is this socially defined behaviour that if you are seen to deviate from it, you are seen in a bad light by your contemporaries: *'Have you noticed how John never buys his round of drinks!'*

In reality, the power of this social construct is profound, and without being aware of it we all experience its influence on our behaviour regularly! Consider the following examples (that you have probably experienced yourself). A waiter gives you fabulous attentive and personalised service in a restaurant... instead of begrudging the fact that you are 'expected' to tip him you actually *want* to tip him. You may even try to slip him a tip quietly, just to make sure that it goes into his pocket (reciprocity in action)! A colleague offers to cover your shift at work when an emergency comes up. Who do you think is the first to offer to step in and help him out when he is in need of a favour (reciprocity in action)?

Powerless to resist

One of the most impressive examples I know of the power of reciprocity involved a friend of mine. He lost his wallet when out on a walk. An hour or so later, just as he was about to start cancelling his credit cards, he received a phone call. Someone had found his wallet while walking his dog. He looked through the wallet, found my friend's business card and gave him a call. My friend was absolutely delighted and asked when he could come and pick it up. The caller said that he was not to worry, he had seen my friend's address on the business card and he would be happy to drop it in later that day... Wow, how kind. True to his word, a couple of hours later he arrived at my friend's house, wallet in hand. My friend thanked him profusely, looked inside his wallet to find that nothing was missing, pulled out a £20 note and offered it as a token of his appreciation (reciprocity in action). To his surprise, Rob (the guy's name) refused the gesture, stating that he hoped that someone would do the same for him if he lost his own wallet. At that point my friend said the following: '*OK, that's very kind of you (pause). If there's anything I can do to help you out in the future, just let me know. You know where I live.*' My friend bid Rob farewell, closed the door and went back to his life; after a while the whole incident went out of his mind.

That was until a Sunday afternoon a few weeks later. My friend was having a late Sunday lunch with his family when there was an unexpected ring on the doorbell. He answered the door to find Rob standing there! Somewhat surprised and slightly bemused, he greeted Rob and asked what he could do for him. This is what Rob said to him: *I'm really sorry to call on you out of the blue and bother you on a Sunday afternoon and I wouldn't have done so had I not exhausted all other options, but I remember you saying that if you could ever help me out to let you know.*'

My friend let out a rather apprehensive, *'Yes?'* Rob continued, *'Well, my wife is arriving at the airport in just over an hour and is expecting me to be there to collect her. My car has broken down, I have called around everyone that I know to see whether they can help me out but I can't get in touch with anyone. With time running short I remembered your kind offer. I'm really sorry to put you in this position and I understand if you can't help but is there any chance you could run me up to the airport... now?'* My friend paused, thought, stuttered a bit, but eventually said, *'Err, yes (cough) I suppose so!'* And with that, walked back in to his house, explained the situation to his wife and took Rob to the airport to collect his wife, the whole round trip taking the best part of three hours! (RECIPROCITY IN ACTION)

I wouldn't have done that!

For any of you reading this thinking there is no way you would have been as stupid as my friend, just consider how difficult it would have been to turn down someone in need who had previously done such a good deed for you. You may not have gone as far as my friend, maybe making up some kind of excuse as to why you would love to help but are unable, but you would have felt the emotional and social obligation to do so and having said no, you would probably have felt quite guilty about it

> Just consider how difficult it would have been to turn down someone in need who had previously done such a good deed for you.

and would probably have continued thinking about Rob, whether his wife made it home, what his opinion of you and the way you reneged on your offer was. This all comes under the power of reciprocity.

So, how does reciprocity come into play in the service environment? To understand this we need to get a sense of perspective on what constitutes a 'positive action'. And it's at this stage that I would like to take you right back to the opening of the book where I dealt with the concept of exceeding guests' expectations. To put it simply, when we deliver a level of service that falls in line with what our guests expect we are not generating any kind of reciprocal capital. Even if we meet every expectation they have, all we are actually doing is providing them with the level of service they expect for their money.

However, the moment we go above and beyond that level of expectation we start to move in to the environment where reciprocity flourishes. In this case, the guest starts to feel that the level of service they are experiencing is beyond that which they should expect for their money, that it is more personalised in its application and that the server has gone well beyond what should be expected of them with no motivation for their behaviour other than providing the best experience possible for the guest. The guest therefore experiences a strong sense of reciprocity and a need to reward (or pay back) the giver, over and above having paid their bill. This is often what motivates guests to add larger, more personally targeted tips, beyond the expected 10 per cent service charge. In fact, if you have ever been in the position, as a guest yourself, where you seek out the individual who served you and quietly slip them a £10 note, saying, 'I just wanted to make sure this ended up in your pocket', then you have yourself been responding to the 'law' of reciprocity. You received unexpectedly good service and wanted to reward/pay back the person responsible personally.

By understanding this dynamic, you should also be able to see the value of the Ultimate Bartender's ethos. Do everything you can to deliver the very best experience possible, whether it is personalising service, making amazing recommendations, constructing great drinks, dealing with challenging situations, etc. In doing so, the Ultimate Bartender is not simply setting the highest standards of serve or delivering the most amazing experiences, he is also creating the environment where reciprocity breathes.

> **By understanding this dynamic, you should also be able to see the value of the Ultimate Bartender's ethos.**

And how do the Ultimate Bartender's guests repay the deed? Well, increased tips is one example, but in terms of 'repayment', their reciprocal actions can also further enhance their own experience.

Consider this example:

You make a great recommendation using all the communication skills covered in the earlier part of this chapter. The guest experiences a sense of focused, preferential, tailored service that results in an immediate repayment with the guest rewarding your efforts by accepting your recommendation (reciprocity situation number 1). As a consequence, having accepted your recommendation, the guest's experience has been enhanced further with the introduction to a drink that they would never have found without you (reciprocity situation number 2). Once again, the guest responds with a payment of trust, *'OK, that was great, I'm in your hands now, what do you recommend next?'* You produce more suggestions, maybe some for his friends too, each one being a new or enhanced experience (reciprocity situation number 3). Ultimately, the final reciprocity payment would come in the form of a parting tip, loyalty to your bar (they return often) or the spreading of your reputation. Whichever way, by creating a reciprocal environment through the delivery of Ultimate Bartender style service, you benefit, the guest benefits and the business benefits. Win-Win-Win ☺

TAKEAWAYS FROM THIS CHAPTER

- Remember that your communication skills are your single biggest asset when becoming an Ultimate Bartender. The more work you put into developing them, the better you will become. The best Ultimate Bartenders are the strongest communicators too.

- 'Sizzle' your recommendations to elicit the biggest emotional response from your guests.

- Always consider the role of the limbic system and how it works. You can then make sure that you are using the most effective 'language' to communicate your messages.

- Remember the 7%-38%-55% communication model of Albert Mehrabian and try to avoid simply relying on 'what you say'. Your body language and vocal skills make all the difference to what you communicate and how it is received.

- Link your improved communication skills to the process of creating an environment of reciprocity with your guests. The combination of the two will prove almost irresistible to them.

CHAPTER 11

Understanding that It's Never Personal

In this chapter, we discover how to deal with busy bars and rude guests and how to turn negative situations into positive ones.

The bar and hospitality environment is without doubt a highly pressurised and stressful one. It is one of the few industries where your guests are mostly, to some degree, under the influence of alcohol. This of course can make for a great atmosphere, but it can also lead to overemotional, unreasonable behaviour, sometimes aggression and even violence. The Ultimate Bartender is a master of recognising and dealing with these situations and here we will outline a variety of approaches and techniques that they use. Not only to diffuse situations but often to completely reverse them, turning a potential negative into an ultimate positive.

....

Dealing with difficult or challenging guests is, well, challenging! Often, we are required to possess a thick skin, put up with behaviour that we would never accept in our private lives or, on occasion, find ourselves having to deal with the sort of people that we would avoid like the plague in our private lives.

However, the biggest barrier to our ability to deal with these situations comes not from a specific lack of training in conflict resolution but something more fundamental than that. It's our propensity to take their behaviour personally. To assume that in some way their behaviour is a personal attack of some sort. In doing so, we become exposed to the range of emotional reactions that can render us vulnerable in the very moment we need to be calm, unemotional and sensitive to what the situation requires from us in terms of a satisfactory resolution.

In doing so, we become exposed to the range of emotional reactions that can render us vulnerable in the very moment we need to be calm.

When working with groups of hospitality staff, I often pose the question, 'Who's ever been upset or wound up by one of your guests?' Generally, everyone has at least one experience of this. So, we then get into various activities that outline the situations and circumstances that left them feeling 'wounded' and further explore why it was that, in their particular experiences, the guests had managed to get under their skin and upset them.

Generally, responses tend to fall into one of the following categories.

The guest ...

- Was rude to them personally
- Was insulting

- Had a bad attitude
- Was too drunk and aggressive
- Spoke down to them
- Was verbally abusive
- Was physically abusive
- Was sexist
- Was racist

The list goes on.

With each example, the bartender has been upset, angered, frightened, insulted or belittled by this behaviour, and as a result has responded in a variety of ways, none of which has resulted in a satisfactory end game.

It is at this stage that I need to remind you of the ultimate goal of running a hospitality business. Namely, to make our guests happy. That is, to make *all* our guests happy *all* of the time. At least, that's the aim. And when we say all guests, we have to take into account that not everyone that walks into our bar is going to be the perfect, polite and appreciative person that we would like. In fact, if we were only in business to serve the 'nicest' people, our bars and restaurants would be pretty empty most of the time. Therefore, instead of being upset and surprised by challenging guests, we should instead have the frame of mind that says, 'We are in the business of providing a service for all guests, including the most challenging ones, and we consider the most polite and appreciative ones to be a nice bonus rather than the expected norm.' In doing so, we set ourselves on the path to developing a mindset that embraces the challenges provided by imperfect guests as part of our role rather than considering them an unwelcoming side of a job that we would ordinarily love if only everyone were nice!

Just another opportunity to demonstrate your skills

In fact, when it comes to dealing with challenging guests, our ability to do so should be viewed as yet another of the skills possessed by the Ultimate Bartender. As a young bartender, it was always my belief that I fell into the Ultimate Bartender category, that I was at the top of my game and at the top of the bartending tree. Accordingly, when faced with challenging guests, I never took their behaviour personally. I never became upset, angry or irritated by

> **I always viewed their behaviour as a challenge to my skills.**

anyone, no matter how awfully they may have behaved. Instead, I always viewed their behaviour as a challenge to my skills. So much so that if I ever let a guest get to me emotionally, I would consider my reaction as an indictment of my skill level. In other words, maybe I was not as talented as I thought! Maybe I needed to work on developing these skills further, and in doing so, over time, I became very good at dealing with the most awkward and challenging guests. To the point where I could often transform a situation from an overtly negative one into an eminently positive one. It is true to say that, over the years, some of my most loyal and valued guests have started off as quite unwelcome indeed.

So, how do we achieve this state of mind? How do we protect ourselves from all the negative feelings and reactions we experience when dealing with guests of this type? Well, it all starts with one simple but incredibly powerful premise: *It's Never Personal.*

That's it: no matter what a guest says or does, it is never personal. And if it's not personal then it can't bother or upset you. Consider this:

Would you be upset if a guest insulted you? If yes, why? Is it because you value their opinion?

It's not the real you

The Ultimate Bartender understands something critical and fundamental here. Namely, how can you value the negative opinion of a guest who doesn't know you or, for that matter, you don't know? Just to be clear, I don't mean they are necessarily a stranger to you, but in truth, they only know the professional version of you and not the one that should matter to you personally, namely the real person you are in your private life. Therefore, if they don't know you, why should their insult carry any weight with you? By responding personally and emotionally you are suggesting that this guest, this stranger to you, this person who knows nothing about the real you, is nevertheless someone whose comments and attitude you value. Otherwise, why would it bother you?

During my bartending career, whenever faced with this kind of situation, I would always remind myself that the opinions that I care about are those of my friends and family, that the guest I was faced with in a difficult moment was simply that, a guest behaving poorly. Beyond my being the bartender looking after them in that moment, they knew nothing about anything that truly mattered to me in my private life and as a consequence their insult was of no consequence whatsoever to me from a personal perspective. However, from a professional one it was always a challenge to my skills. Could I diffuse this situation? Can I calm things down? Can I turn this person around? Can I make them happy? Had I, even for one moment, become emotional about the situation, then the answers to those questions would have been 'no'. However, by allowing insults to bounce off me, I was able to apply myself to the situation in a professional manner, to see beyond the moment and focus on what I needed to do to transform the situation from negative to positive.

I was able to focus on what I needed to do to transform the situation from negative to positive.

In fact, there was nothing that I enjoyed more than having a guest come to me at the end of an evening, having behaved really poorly at some stage, and say, 'Thanks for a great night and sorry that I was behaving like such an idiot earlier on.' Whenever this happened (and it happened on numerous occasions over the years) I would feel amazing. It was confirmation that I was really good at this job, that I had all the skills of an Ultimate Bartender.

Easier said than done

While it sounds simple, it can certainly be a challenge to make the necessary psychological shift that I am referring to. To move from a position where you are susceptible to having your buttons pushed by anyone to wearing the metaphorical suit of armour that will render you immune to the daily onslaught of random guests and their diverse personalities and behaviours can be significant. However, as with other topics in this book, it all comes down to possessing a specific Ultimate Bartender mindset, one that defines you as being amongst the most talented and rounded bartenders in the industry.

To help you achieve this required state of mind you will need to have a clear point of differentiation between your personal and professional self. To recognise that while you bring elements of your personal self to your job role, the professional version is not who you are in your personal life. There should be significant differences in terms of attitude, projection of personality, role priorities, the nature of relationship building, and of course the broader range of people and personality types, compared to your personal life, that you are looking to develop rapport with.

Thinking like an actor

I tend to feel that the best example I can give you of this state of mind is that of an actor. In many respects, there are numerous parallels between the approach of an actor and that of the Ultimate Bartender. Both are dedicated to the delivery of an entertainment experience and both 'play' a role. For the actor, however, when they are in character, the difference between their personal and work self is quite clear. They are essentially pretending to be someone else. And while you may at first believe this is a more extreme departure than that of the Ultimate Bartender, you are in fact mistaken. For the Ultimate Bartender, like the actor, is also 'playing' a role; it is the role of the Ultimate Bartender and it is no closer to the real person than is the case with an actor. Because, as is the case with the Ultimate Bartender, the actor draws on his own real-life experiences and personality traits to help shape the character they are playing. The main difference between the two is that the actor clearly identifies that when in character they are not their personal self, whereas many bartenders aspiring to become *Ultimate* struggle to differentiate between the two.

So, think of yourself as a performer, consider the bar your stage (more of this in the final chapter) and think of your guests as your audience. Think of your working shift as the time that you are in character. You are not your personal self but instead playing the role of the Ultimate Bartender, bringing all of your high-end skills to bear on the Ultimate Bartending performance. As with the actor, all of your personal issues are left in the wings and the moment you step on to your stage you leave them all aside, to be picked up again once you step off the stage and leave your audience behind. If you have ever visited the theatre, you will notice that the actor never gives any sense of anything that may be bothering them; if the audience doesn't respond in the desired way it has no effect on their performance. They don't take it personally, get upset or start reacting defensively to the audience. They simply remain professional, focusing on delivering the best performance with the singular goal of sending the audience away happy. The Ultimate Bartender is essentially an actor performing on a different type of stage and with a diverse and more fluid audience. If you can therefore start thinking in this vein, it will help you to hold on to the perspective that you require to master the *It's Never Personal* mindset.

Using empathy

It always makes me smile when I hear the following words, *'I understand what you're saying, but...'* In a service context, that small, critical 'but' is a precursor to revealing that by giving a different opinion/outlook/view, etc. you don't <u>truly</u> understand or accept that person's view or opinion. In a service environment, when dealing with challenging situations, this can be disastrous. It instantly kills rapport (if you had it in the first place), undermines any level of trust you had worked hard to build, and potentially belittles your guest (depending on their levels of pride or self-confidence), which all leads to the likelihood of an unhappy outcome. True empathy, particularly in a service environment, is a rare and powerful thing that ultimately comes down to attitude, perspective and phraseology. It's also true to say any bartender who displays a general lack of empathy in life is also unlikely to use this key skill at work.

> **True empathy, particularly in a service environment, is a rare and powerful thing.**

How empathetic are you?

Consider this scenario that I have used when talking to groups about road rage:

You are driving along the motorway in the centre lane at 70mph, a good distance from the car ahead, 800 yards from the upcoming junction, happily minding your own business. Suddenly a Porsche 911 in the outside lane cuts across you, narrowly missing the front of your car. You have to brake suddenly. The driver then cuts to the inside lane and disappears off at the next junction without an apparent care in the world for what he has just done!

How do you react?

a. Slow down, watch him rush off into the distance and happily continue with your journey?

b. Hoot your horn, flash your headlights and shout a few words questioning his parentage?

c. Chase him off the motorway, run him off the road, drag him from his car, take the Colt 45 from your glove box and shoot him in the back of his head?!

In years past, I certainly would have answered 'b', on occasions bordering on a 'c'. However, in my more mature incarnation I would definitely answer 'a'. And that's not because I have mellowed with age (countless people of my generation and older suffer intensely from road rage); it's because I have managed to develop my empathy skills. So, these days, when I'm on the receiving end of a potential road-rage incident, I take a deep breath and remind myself of the following...

For each driver on the road who cuts across me, who pulls out in front of me when there is not enough space, who pushes in front of me in a queue, who drives too close to my rear on a motorway, who jumps a roundabout or anything else for that matter, I know that I have done similar to someone else. I have been the perpetrator on as many occasions as I have been the victim. And, when I have been the one forcing someone to slam on their brakes, why have I done that? What I can tell you is why I *haven't* done it. I haven't done it to upset a complete stranger or to put their (and my) safety at risk. I may have driven badly because I wasn't concentrating (easy to do when you spend as much time in a car as I do), or maybe I was unfamiliar with where I was and found myself in the wrong lane and needed to make a last-minute change. Maybe it was because a car was sitting in my blind spot and I thought I was clear of it, maybe it was one of a hundred other reasons that were about no more than the fallibility of being human. What I know is that, if like me, you drive a car you will have been in the same situation yourself.

So why is it that when we are the perpetrator of the action we feel we simply made a mistake and that the angry person in the other car is being unreasonable in their response? And yet, when we are on the receiving end we can be unforgiving, angry and react as if the other driver has committed an unforgiveable sin? This is a lack of empathy on our part. We react, jump to the worst-case scenario conclusion. We have no time for excuses and base our reaction on a set of standards that we set for others while having excuses for ourselves in the same situation. So, when I am on the receiving end, instead of getting angry and aggressive I simply remind myself of the many reasons that may lead me to do the same thing myself, and assume the other driver may also have any one of those understandable and acceptable reasons for having done so. At which point it is so much easier to just let the incident pass me by. I have quite simply tried to put myself in the other person's shoes.

Think now about all the guests who have upset or angered you at work at some point. Here are a few scenarios that may resonate:

- Guest insulted you because they weren't happy with something.

- Guest was loud and abusive because they had drunk too much.

- Guest 'instructed' you (like a servant) rather than requested.

- Guest raised their voice (or shouted) at you.

On the surface this appears to be unacceptable behaviour on the part of the guest. After all, would you accept being treated like this in your private life? However, if you can avoid reacting instinctively and instead take that (metaphorical) deep breath and ask yourself, 'Could there be something else behind this other than what it appears? Could their behaviour be for a reason other than they are just being rude to me?' Then you begin to leverage the power of empathy in your favour and to the ultimate benefit of the guest.

> **Then you begin to leverage the power of empathy in your favour and to the ultimate benefit of the guest.**

Let's take the first example I gave above: The guest insulted you because they weren't happy with something. Here are some options for reasons explaining their behaviour:

- They have had one of those days when everything has gone wrong for them and your tiny error was the straw that broke the camel's back.

- They were sacked from their job that day.

- They had just had a huge argument with their partner.

- Their wallet had been stolen that afternoon.

I could go on and on. The point is that it could have been anything. Let's face it, how many times have we all had a really bad day and taken it out on someone for the slightest little thing? In every case, the guest's behaviour, although aimed at you, was not about you at all.

When all is said and done, we simply don't know why people behave the way they do in any given moment. Because the nature of the hospitality industry is such that our interaction with our guest is just a momentary snapshot of their life, we can't know what came before for them. And that could have been absolutely anything. If instead of reacting to that momentary interaction in isolation we instead ask ourselves, *Could there be something else going on here?*, while we can't know for sure, this approach gives us a sense of perspective, protects us from the sensitivities of being on the receiving end of apparent poor behaviour and enables us to focus on the Ultimate Bartender's ultimate goal: to make the guests happy.

Remember, each time you become emotionally impacted, your ability to achieve the goal of a happy guest is undermined dramatically. For most, it becomes impossible.

How do people make empathy work for them?

Here's an example from a different industry that shines a light on the powerful use of empathy in getting past negativity. A salesman attending one of my rapport-building courses (let's call him Harry) was suffering as a result of a negative public attitude towards the company he worked for. It was an attitude based on historic poor experiences and, regardless of the fact that the company had transformed its products, management style, sales force and dedication to customer service, far too often he experienced rejection purely based on public perception of the company. Harry's response was to defend his employers, citing all the positives while explaining how much they had changed in the last ten years. In fact, Harry was saying pretty much the same things (he thought) as Rahim, one of his colleagues, but for some reason Rahim was making many times more sales than Harry. So what was Harry's problem? What was the difference between the approach of Harry and Rahim? You've got it... Empathy. When faced with a customer who wasn't interested in doing business with him because of their negative view or experiences with his company, Harry would respond by saying, 'Yes, we used to be like that but we have changed a lot since then, for example....'

Woah! Where's the empathy Harry?

Walk a mile in someone else's shoes
Anon

A famous proverb but, as with so many, we rarely stop to consider the wisdom of it.

In our example, Harry was missing a fantastic opportunity to develop rapport and trust through the use of empathy. Harry was showing no interest in his customer's past bad experience ('Oh dear, what happened?'). There was no acknowledgement that he could understand why they felt the way they did ('Ah yes, if that had happened to me I'd feel the same way as you do.'). And did you notice the disastrous 'but' word in there? The red flag that says, 'I'm not really listening to what you are saying, I just want to tell you why you are wrong.'

It is important to realise that:

People like to be listened to.
People like to be given the time to air their views.
People like to be understood, and most importantly...
People like to feel the effects of EMPATHY.

A typical response from Rahim in the same situation would include something along these lines: 'Oh dear, have you had a bad experience with us in the past?' 'Tell me what happened.' 'That's awful, I'm not surprised you feel the way you do.' Anything to let them blow off some steam and feel that they had an ally in Rahim. Only once he had used empathy to build trust and rapport would Rahim then respond (not react) with something like, 'Well, I think you'll be pleased to know that it is because of the experiences customers like yourself endured that ten years ago the board was replaced...' etc. He would then go on to tell them the same positive news about the company that Harry had tried to express.

The main difference between the two salesmen was that Harry, who was in too much of a hurry to explain why his customer's views were out-dated, demonstrated no empathy whatsoever, resulting in non-existent rapport, low levels of trust and ultimately very low sales conversions. While Rahim, who was a naturally empathetic salesman, achieved very impressive sales results under the same conditions.
And this example of the two salesmen provides the perfect analogy for the difference between the average bartender and the

multi-talented Ultimate Bartender. Our Ultimate Bartender understands the value of empathy in all aspects of his work. Whether it is within the context of this chapter's subject or whether it relates to upselling, recommendation, hosting skills or heads-up bartending, the ability to empathise with our fellow human beings makes it far easier to develop relationships, build rapport and trust, and influence people's lives positively while remaining relaxed and focused throughout.

The ability to empathise with our fellow human beings makes it far easier to develop relationships, build rapport and trust.

The good news is that you can develop your empathetic side. As with all the skills in this book, and as I have repeated on numerous occasions now, it's simply a matter of practice. In future, try to resist the urge to react or defend, desperately seeking the quick positive response. Instead look for the opportunities to demonstrate to your guests that you truly understand them and that you are an ally and not an enemy. Put yourself in their 'shoes' and imagine how you would feel in their position. In doing so, you will start to harness an invaluable skill that will underpin your approach to all challenging situations. It will relax you when under pressure and feed your levels of confidence when you most need it. Become the empathetic *actor* and you will have created one of the most powerful foundations for Ultimate Bartending.

TAKEAWAYS FROM THIS CHAPTER

- Realise that having to deal with negative behaviours or rude guests is never personal, no matter how it may appear. Think of these situations as part of your job role and a challenge to your skill base.

- Remember that guests are not your personal friends. They only know the professional version of you and therefore cannot impact the personal, private YOU!

- When dealing with a rude guest, ask yourself, 'Do I value their opinion?' This mantra can help you keep a clear professional perspective when under pressure.

- Think like an actor and play the role. You can draw on your personal experiences but leave the private, personal YOU in the wings.

- Focus on employing empathy in situations where it can be difficult to be empathetic. By looking for the empathetic position, you protect yourself from knee-jerk reactions to negative situations and are also protected from personal, emotional responses.

CHAPTER 12

Realising that It's All in the Mind

In this chapter we discover how to turn stressful work experiences into self-motivating challenges.

Outside of the potential for difficult guests, the hospitality environment is a naturally pressurised one regardless. Bartenders often suffer from stress in the workplace, which in turn has an impact on their ability to do their job well and enjoy the experience of doing so. This then has a direct impact on the guest experience as they in turn 'feel' the bartender's stress and react to it accordingly. This in turn feeds the stress further. In this chapter we deal with the subject of workplace stress, what it is, what triggers it, and provide different techniques and psychological perspectives to help lessen or even eradicate it completely.

....

What is stress?

The Mental Health Foundation describes stress as follows:

Stress can be defined as the way you feel when you're under abnormal pressure.

All sorts of situations can cause stress. The most common involve work, money matters and relationships with partners, children or other family members. Stress may be caused either by major upheavals and life events such as divorce, unemployment, moving house and bereavement, or by a series of minor irritations such as feeling undervalued at work or dealing with difficult children. Sometimes there are no obvious causes.

Some stress can be positive. Research shows that a moderate level of stress makes us perform better. It also makes us more alert and can help us perform better in situations such as job interviews or public speaking. Stressful situations can also be exhilarating and some people actually thrive on the excitement that comes with dangerous sports or other high-risk activities.

But stress is only healthy if it is short-lived. Excessive or prolonged stress can lead to illness and physical and emotional exhaustion. Taken to extremes, stress can be a killer.

We all experience stress to some degree or another, but for many of us it can exceed the 'moderate' level described above and can start to impact negatively on our lives, health and mental state.

Living in the future

I like to describe the feeling of stress in its negative form as worrying about the future. Worrying about something that is yet to occur. In this case, the future could be next year, next week or in twenty seconds' time. For example, a bartender who is struggling to keep up with the number of guests at the bar on a Friday night might stress about the next person he has to serve. For example, the guest may look irritated at having to wait, he may look like the sort of person that is going to complain or be abusive. This worry about what is going to happen in the future (in a few moments' time) can easily cause stress for the bartender.

> **This worry about what is going to happen in the future (in a few moments' time) can easily cause stress for the bartender.**

When I was a young bartender I was quite familiar with the feeling of stress. I enjoyed serving guests and making cocktails but would get stressed about so many situations. If the number of people at the bar began to swell and I could sense them becoming impatient about having to wait, if they were getting a bit too drunk and starting to behave aggressively, if the chef was in a bad mood, if my boss was criticising my work, if... etc.

I remember one occasion on a beautiful sunny day when the bar I was working in was packed out; we didn't have enough bartenders working that shift so the pressure was already on. Guests were having to wait far too long for their drinks and the atmosphere around the bar wasn't great! We were selling bottled beers so quickly that the ones we were re-stocking the fridges with didn't have enough time to chill and so the guests were complaining about warm beer. And then, just when things were far from good, catastrophe struck: the ice machine broke down!

No ice, no cocktails, no cold drinks, disaster! Our guests were furious and generally unforgiving. People were refusing to pay for their drinks and their anger was directed at us, the bartenders. I remember my stress levels had gone through the roof. I just wanted to turn and leave the bar. I actually felt quite sick.

By the end of the shift, I was ready to pack it in. I was truly considering whether being a bartender was the career for me. It just didn't seem to be worth the hassle, the worry, the stress. This was all prior to my *heads-up* experience as described in chapter 5.

With the doors finally closed and the last guest long gone I found myself mopping the floor with an intense sense of relief that it was all over. My manager could see that I was a bit shell-shocked; he had seen me struggling throughout service. He told me to put the mop down and to come and join him for a quick beer. I propped the mop against the bar, wandered over, sat down with a slump and picked up the beer. 'Cheers,' he said. 'That was fun, wasn't it'? 'Not really,' I replied. He then said, 'Let me give you a little tip.' He went on to say something that entirely changed my perspective on the things that I worried about. Not simply in work but also in life.

Wise words on perspective

He said to me that I should think back over the shift about every little thing that I was worrying about. To think about each occasion that I worried about the atmosphere in the bar, when a guest complained, when the ice machine broke, when the beers were warm, when service was slow because there were too many guests to serve.

He then asked me to think about how I was now, in this moment. Was I well? Did I get through the shift to the best of my ability? Had the experience had a negative effect on my life? For example, had it changed my friends and family, the place I lived, the things I love to do, the holiday I'm going on next month? Or, was life just going to carry on as normal? He told me that 'shit happened', that whatever the situation, I could only do my best. He then explained that the only thing that I had achieved by worrying was to feel stressed. It hadn't changed the situation; it had only made me feel rubbish throughout it. And now that it was over, it was consigned to history and simply wasn't worth worrying about either now or then. Sure, I could learn from it; it was an experience after all and it would prepare me for when something similar happened again. However, he also told me that if I really thought about it, did any of the things that I was worrying about really turn out to be as bad as I thought they would? We had a challenging situation, we did the best that we could, there were many unhappy guests but ultimately it was just one of those things. Certainly nowhere near as bad as I had been anticipating throughout the experience. He then said this: 'Yesterday's history, tomorrow's a mystery. Live in the moment, don't worry about what has passed and certainly don't worry about an imagined future.' This philosophy has shaped my attitude to life, work and stress ever since.

The Power of Now

In his book *The Power of NOW*, Eckhart Tolle describes the futility of living your life in a fantasy future. He explains that whatever we imagine the future to be it is almost never the case. He suggests thinking back over the course of your life and considering all the situations that you worried about in advance, and then asking yourself, Were they ever as bad as you had imagined? Did you get through them? Looking back, apart from making you feel bad at the time, what role did the stress play in helping you to eventually cope with the situation when it arrived? Again, looking back, had you not been imagining and worrying about the future, but instead had just lived in the moment, would you have still coped with the situation when it arrived, in whatever form it did?

An ability to just live in the NOW and not in your imagined future has the remarkable impact of reducing, sometimes completely eliminating, the stresses that you experience. I can't imagine the terror of being taken hostage by a terrorist group where the potential for stress caused by the constant imagining of the road ahead, what the final outcome might be, must be unimaginable. And yet, when people who have been successfully freed from similar dreadful situations are interviewed about their experiences, it becomes clear what their survival strategies often were. They talk about taking one day at a time, trying never to think about what may lie ahead but instead just focusing on the moment they were in. As remarkable at this seems, it is the same psychological approach that we can all adopt when dealing with the rather more mundane stresses that we experience in our daily work lives.

So, next time you are starting to feel the stresses of work getting on top of you, try to do the same. Actively block out any thoughts or worries about what may happen; just focus on doing the best that you can in the moment, take the attitude that as and when a situation presents itself you will deal with it to the best of your ability in that moment and that you won't distract and stress yourself by worrying about what might happen in advance.

As with every skill in this book, becoming skilled at this is a matter of practice. It is also a life philosophy. So, would you like to live your life as I describe, without worrying unnecessarily? If so, there is nothing stopping you. It is simply a choice. Your choice. Just choose to do it and you will find that the more you do so, the better you will become at it. Before you know it, you will recognise that the things that have historically been a cause of stress to you have begun to disappear. You will also notice that you begin to view those situations as positive challenges that you welcome and embrace as part of your journey to becoming an Ultimate Bartender.

> **Actively block out any thoughts or worries about what may happen; just focus on doing the best that you can in the moment.**

TAKEAWAYS FROM THIS CHAPTER

- Remember that stress is generally a fear or worry about something that is yet to occur. Instead of worrying about what may happen in the future, focus on what is happening in the NOW.

- Think back over past stressful situations to help you gain a sense of perspective. In other words, when you look back, was it really as bad as you had feared?

- Remember that yesterday is history, tomorrow's a mystery.

- Consider the stressful challenges of work part of the job rather than an unwelcome hindrance. By doing so, you will be better equipped to embrace the things that cause you stress as opposed to hoping that they don't occur.

- Consider reading Eckhart Tolle's *The Power of NOW*. His book has changed the lives of tens of millions of people and can help provide a significantly more in-depth perspective on mindfulness and how to deal with the stresses we encounter in our lives.

CHAPTER 13

Performing: The Theatre of Bartending

This chapter considers how to develop, brand and project your unique style and personality.

We have already discovered how Ultimate Bartenders work as part of an effective team. However, this doesn't mean that they are clones of one another. Here it is important to distinguish between the self-obsessed, ego-driven non-team member and the unique style and personality of the individual within the team. Think of this as your personal brand. In the same way, a company can have distinct, powerful brands (in their own right) as part of a large portfolio. Likewise, a successful bar team can have talented, entertaining and diverse personalities with unique bartending styles as part of a powerful brand (your place of work). Here we look at developing your personal style, playing to your personality strengths, how you present yourself on the bar and how you impact the team while developing your own unique brand.

• • • • • • • • • • • • • •

I have always felt that the bartending profession is a form of theatre, with the bartenders themselves being the principal players and the physical bar being the stage. To walk into a bar where there is a buzz around the bartenders, where the guests are engaged in an interactive experience, enjoying a form of entertainment rather than simply having drinks mixed for them by passive servers, is a sight to behold.

When it comes to the Ultimate Bartender, it becomes clear that his extensive range of skills combine to a specific end. The delivery of an amazing service experience that is also a form of entertainment in its own right. We call this approach *The Theatre of Bartending*.

> I have always felt that the bartending profession is a form of theatre, with the bartenders themselves being the principal players and the physical bar being the stage.

For the Ultimate Bartender, everything he does feeds in to this sense of theatre. From handling a glass or picking up a shaker to making a recommendation or greeting a guest with warmth and engagement, it is the minutiae of their range of skills that combine to create unforgettable experiences.

In this section, I am not going to revisit the topics covered in previous chapters; we'll take them as a given. Instead, I want to concentrate here on style, attitude and demeanour. This is the element of bartending that frames the performance: it's the wrapping on a gift, the frosting on a cake. The following list is not exhaustive but will serve to communicate the message that the very smallest considerations to the way in which you present yourself can have the biggest impact on how the guest perceives you.

Projecting your stance

The way that an Ultimate Bartender holds himself is key. It is the opportunity to project passion, confidence and enthusiasm. And yet, without consideration it can project apathy, disinterest, even boredom. Consider how you stand or walk around behind the bar. Avoid slouching or dragging yourself around as if you have weights in your shoes. Think instead of adopting an upright posture with your head held high (not too high, that would be weird!).

Also, think about your shoulders. If they are hanging forward or down somewhat, this tends to project a negative state such as disinterest or lack of enthusiasm. Instead try to be aware of your stance and if you notice that you are slouching, have a stretch and pull your shoulders back a little. Often, fatigue due to being on your feet for long periods can result in hanging shoulders. It may not be the case that you are feeling negative but the slouched shoulders will still project it. Likewise, think about what you are doing with your hands. Things to avoid are crossing your arms when addressing a guest, standing with hands in pockets or rubbing your face. Alternatively, keeping your hands free and visible, gesturing when appropriate, projects positivity and helps communicate expressively.

Checking and holding glasses

The way in which an Ultimate Bartender handles glassware often differentiates him from many bartenders. He understands a few critical facts here. Firstly, the glass is going to hold the guest's drink; the guest is going to drink from it. As a consequence, the Ultimate Bartender's hands avoid going anywhere near the rim of the glass. In fact, the general rule is that the bartender should handle the bottom third of the glass only, while the remaining two thirds belong to the guest. Next, the Ultimate Bartender will always check the condition of the glass, making sure it is perfectly clean, the correct temperature (not warm from the glasswasher) and that it has no chips or cracks. This also provides an opportunity for theatre. By confidently holding the glass up to the light (sometimes with a flourish) and checking the glass in full view of the guest, the Ultimate Bartender is also making a statement. He is demonstrating his style (the flourish), his professionalism, his standards (I want to make sure this glass is in perfect condition to hold your drink), and is communicating that the process of checking the glass is an essential element of the drink-making procedure. This is all in stark contrast to the many bartenders who just grab a glass and start pouring the drink.

Pouring (jigger or free)

Pouring is yet another opportunity that the Ultimate Bartender takes to demonstrate style and confidence while displaying his skills and drink-making prowess. Whether it is wine into a glass, spirits into a jigger, beer, softs or water, they pour with aplomb, avoiding spillage and over-pouring. When it's spirits into a jigger, the jigger is always held directly over the glass so that the moment the measure is full it is instantly dropped into the glass while the pour is simultaneously 'cut'. This speeds up service, projects professionalism and avoids the comic balancing act experienced by those bartenders who fill the jigger away from the intended receptacle and then precariously transport it towards the glass in an effort not to spill the precious cargo!

As the Ultimate Bartender becomes more adept at pouring, the entertainment value also increases, with long pours (pouring from a height), slick 'cutting' (stopping the pour) techniques and two-handed pours. Each of these techniques enhances drink-making efficiency while embellishing the entertainment factor.

Shaking

As with pouring, shaking a cocktail is a great opportunity for theatre. Amongst the Ultimate Bartender community, your shaking style is considered your signature. Firstly, we need to consider the reasons why we shake a cocktail. The three main reasons are to mix the ingredients, to chill the mixture and to some extent add a little dilution. It is therefore important to be aware of the final goal when developing your own 'signature'. Shaking with speed and dynamism not only looks impressive (it is often the part of the drink-making process that guests enjoy the most) but it also achieves the mixing goals. Styles vary, but when it comes to theatre, the ones that entertain the most are the ones that make the biggest display.

Of all the world's Ultimate Bartenders, when it comes to shaking with style Stanislav Vadrna has to be the king of the shake. Some years ago, I was invited to Cognac in France as part of an international delegation of mixologists that had been assembled to collaborate on the creation of 'the next great classic Cognac cocktail'. The amount of talent and experience that had been drawn from around the world was staggering. It included Stanislav, who at that stage wasn't particularly well known amongst the established bartending icons. One afternoon, during a rather noisy development session, I noticed a small crowd gathering around one of the mixologists. The work around the room ground to a halt as we all left our stations to see what was going on. It was Stanislav shaking a cocktail. Shaking with a style that none of us had seen before. He described it as being influenced by Far Eastern culture and martial arts. It was indeed something to behold. Stan has since gone on to become one of the world's mixing gurus and has been interviewed countless times on his mixing philosophy and unique 'ninja' style shake. You can look him up on YouTube!

Of course, while Stan has taken shaking style to another level, far too many bartenders miss the opportunity and in doing so also fail to mix their cocktail well. So, check your style and consider the following:

- No slow languid shaking. It doesn't help the drink and makes you look bored in the process.

- Try to avoid shaking out of view. Instead consider the shake the exciting crescendo of the mixing process and one that you want to share with your audience.

- Finally, find an action that works well for you, fits your personality, feels comfortable, looks dynamic and produces great, well-mixed drinks.

Find an action that works well for you, fits your personality, feels comfortable, looks dynamic and produces great, well-mixed drinks.

Communicating through dress sense

The way you present yourself in terms of dress also communicates a message. You either look great or you don't. This is not a comment on what you wear but more about the way you wear it. For example, some establishments demand formal attire with waistcoats and ties while others have no discernible uniform and allow their staff to wear whatever they like. Whatever your dress style, your goal should be to look as slick as you can. If you wear T-shirt and jeans while sporting a mass of facial hair, make sure the hair looks good and not dirty, that your T-shirt doesn't look as though you have worn it to work it three days in a row and that your jeans don't have evidence of last night's dinner plastered all over them. The way you present yourself reflects your attitude to your job. If you don't care about your image it suggests that you probably don't care too much about anything else, including the drinks you make or the guests you serve.

Interacting with your team

Nobody likes a diva. Not the guests that you serve or the colleagues that you work with. Being great at delivering in *The Theatre of Bartending* is not about being the glory-grabbing 'star' who wants to feed his ego by outperforming his colleagues. It is about being a unique character within a coherent, well-oiled machine. Ultimate Bartenders work hard at developing their skills while collaborating with their team. They both learn from them and help develop them. The result from the guest's perspective is an entertaining experience delivered by a united 'cast'. There are unfortunately many ego-driven individuals who work in our industry, but be aware that few if any of them achieve Ultimate Bartender status. The very act of being motivated by one's own agenda creates a barrier to ultimate development, as in most cases people don't like working with them. So, think 'team', think about what you can contribute and how you can benefit as a result and you'll be on the right track to Ultimate Bartender stardom.

A word on avoiding arrogance

While we are on the subject of ego, it's worth mentioning the trap of arrogance. There is a fine line between confidence and arrogance and it's a line that can be easy to step over, especially in the formative stages of a career. The main difference is attitude of mind. There is nothing wrong with being supremely confident in what you do; in fact, a high level of confidence is essential if you are going to achieve your potential. However, when that confidence becomes ego-driven and self-serving, to the point that you look down on others, underestimate their value, overestimate your own skills and importance, and think of yourself as being above those around you (including the guests), then you are at the top of a slippery slope.

I often think of Usain Bolt (the world's fastest ever human) when the subject of arrogance raises its head. Many people consider him an arrogant person, but when you consider his talent and unrivalled achievements, he is in fact remarkably humble. There is no doubt that he possesses staggering levels of confidence, but he is also a humble human being. He is liked by almost everyone he comes into contact with (except some of his competitors), gives to charity, supports countless worthy causes, surrounds himself with the same people he grew up with, shows respect to all and never forgets where he started.

On the other hand, Carl Lewis (another amazing athlete from an earlier era) could be considered as demonstrating a fairly arrogant attitude. His athletic achievements are staggering and in his time he was considered the greatest track and field athlete ever. However, with the emergence of Usain Bolt, he demonstrates a lack of humility in comparison. He is constantly criticising Usain's achievements (and those of other athletes) in a quest to remain the 'greatest ever'. He never has anything positive to say about anything that may undermine his opinion of himself and as a result finds himself in a situation where fewer people like him for it. In my opinion it has definitely undermined his legacy. For the Ultimate Bartender to avoid this trap, confidence should be accompanied by a humble attitude. Remember that you want to possess an *attitude to serve* so that you can be the best *you* possible. That

> **Confidence should be accompanied by a humble attitude.**

people will like you, want to work with you, learn from you and, from the guest's perspective, return to see you over again.

A word on flair bartending

I love the world of *flair bartending*. I remember the first time I saw the film *Cocktail* with Tom Cruise and was spellbound by the bottle-spinning antics of the main stars. I remember also, as a young bartender, practising for hours in an attempt to bring some of the skills I had witnessed into my own bar. Unfortunately, I was never very good at it! These days, flairing has become a distinct discipline of its own. It's a kind of sport, with countless competitions and championships being held around the world. The best flair bartenders train for hours each day, honing their skills, developing new moves and creating the most amazing routines. Some of the very best have full time 'entertainment' contracts to perform in Las Vegas. I have purposely avoided writing on the subject of flair as it is well beyond my area of expertise. But, in the context of theatre it surely can't be ignored. Accordingly, if this is a route that you would like to go down, knock yourself out! Develop your skills, watch videos, attend courses, become a skilled flairer. Many of the world's Ultimate Bartenders have great flair skills. And, if you go down this route, consider it as yet another string to your bow. Use it when it makes sense and will embellish the guest experience, and enjoy the process while doing so.

When it comes to theatre, nothing is out of bounds. If you can take an aspect of your role and make it entertaining, do so.

However, always remember that your guests are different; they will respond to different levels of entertainment in different ways. For example, flair bartending is considered by many guests as fabulously enthralling – indeed some often demand to see it. However, for other guests it is just not appropriate and can make them feel uncomfortable ('I just want a drink and not a display of juggling'). So, always be sensitive to your audience and remember that you are trying to make them all happy. Theatre is not about entertaining yourself; it is about delivering the right form of entertainment for each individual guest.

> **Remember that your guests are different; they will respond to different levels of entertainment in different ways.**

TAKEAWAYS FROM THIS CHAPTER

- Consider the role of the Ultimate Bartender as one of delivering an entertainment experience with the bartender being the central performer.

- Think of every action and interaction as an opportunity to project style, confidence and a sense of wonder.

- Work with your team as a key member of the entertainment cast. Try to avoid working to your own agenda to the detriment of the team (cast) effort.

- Don't confuse confidence and arrogance. Confidence can be endearing and to the greater benefit of your colleagues and guests. Arrogance tends to be to the cost of both.

- Always look to send your audience away feeling entertained. Concentrate on how you are making them feel rather than simply getting on with the mechanics of fulfilling their orders.

CHAPTER 14

All the Bar's a Stage: The Big Show

In this concluding chapter, we look at how to draw all the book's skills together for the ultimate performance.

In the end, everything that we have looked at is part of a script (of sorts). It's not a script that one consigns to memory to be delivered verbatim to all and sundry. It is a script that you can call on, in part or in whole, at any given moment, which gives you the best chance of delivering the finest, personalised and tailored performances for each of your guests. Thinking in these terms allows us to vary the experience, never being predictable, always potentially offering a distinct experience and consistently exceeding expectations. Here I close with a personal experience, where the server demonstrated use of the wide range of skills covered within this book and in doing so delivered my most impressive service experience bar none.

....

In 2007 I attended a works' reunion. Up until that point I had always shied away from events of that kind, mainly because I had stayed in touch with the people I wanted to and therefore the idea of a reunion never really appealed to me. Nevertheless, on this occasion curiosity got the better of me and I decided to attend. It had been the best part of twenty years since I had seen everyone and as I walked in and looked around I realised that I didn't really recognise anybody. In fact, for a moment I thought I had attended the wrong event. And then, just as I was considering whether to stay, I recognised someone in the far corner of the room. It was Dave, one of my first managers and someone who was a genuinely positive influence on me during the earlier part of my career. I went and joined Dave and we spent the rest of the evening chatting, reminiscing and drinking. Drinking a lot!

Hanging!

The following morning, I awoke with what I can only describe as a twenty-year-old's hangover. The sort of headache and sense of regret that I hadn't experienced since I was in my twenties. It was a Sunday morning and so I dragged myself out of bed and threw myself in the shower. As I was starting to become more lucid, I began thinking about the previous night and how enjoyable it had been catching up with Dave. And then something suddenly dawned on me. Dave had been telling me about this amazing restaurant that had a fantastic selection of whiskies. We had agreed to meet there for a malt or two the next day (today), at lunchtime. I checked my watch, realised that I needed to get moving, jumped out of the shower, got dressed and left to catch a cab. As I pulled up at the restaurant I could see that Dave was waiting for me outside and he was looking as rough as I felt. He greeted me with, 'I'm not sure if we are up for this,' but we entered the restaurant nevertheless.

We were met at the door by an enthusiastic young woman who led us to a table near the bar, gave us a couple of drinks menus and told us that our server would be with us in a moment. Dave and I sat in silence, staring through the menus rather than at them, both wondering what we were doing looking at a drinks menu in the state we were in.

The Ultimate Waitress

A few moments later, as promised, our server arrived. She was a youngish woman full of energy. She stopped, looked at us with a slightly quizzical stare, assessing the situation, and then asked, 'Heavy night last night?' We grunted a response in the affirmative, to which she replied, 'OK, let me make this easy for you, put your menus down.' We obliged.

> **She stopped, looked at us with a slightly quizzical stare, assessing the situation, and then asked, 'Heavy night last night?'**

The conversation then unfolded like this:

Her: 'Right, are you here for the whiskies?'

Us: 'Yes'.

Her: 'Great, because we have a fantastic range of whiskies. And our bartender has created some amazing ways of enjoying them. Do you have any preferences in terms of whisky style?'

Us: [Remembering the old days sharing quite a few] 'Yes, we both enjoy a nice smoky Islay.'

Her: 'Excellent, because if you like Islay, I think you'll love what our bartender can do with a delicious Lagavulin. Let me explain. It comes in three stages. Firstly, I will bring you the bartender's signature palate cleanser. This is a refreshing non-alcoholic drink designed to refresh your senses and prepare you for the sensory assault of the Lagavulin. If you have never done this before, I can assure you that you will experience more from the Lagavulin when you get to it than you can imagine.

'Next, I will bring you the whisky accompanied by small pieces of 100 per cent dark chocolate. This is what you do. Take a piece of the dark chocolate and allow it to melt in your mouth. Just as the bitterness of the chocolate begins to become apparent, take a sip of the whisky. The balance of flavours is amazing, like oral Nirvana. Finally, when you have finished the whisky and the chocolate, I'll bring you a measure each of Balvenie Doublewood. It's not an Islay whisky but the intense notes of caramel and vanilla, especially after the Lagavulin/chocolate, will explode on your tongue. This is an experience not to be missed, we call it the Speylay Explosion.'

Us: [Open-mouthed, drooling somewhat and now having forgotten about our hangovers] 'We'll have two of those!'

And so off she went. First came the delicious non-alcoholic

cocktail, a perfect palate cleanser and much needed to boot. The moment that we were done with those, she was back with the whisky and chocolate. She stayed with us to make sure we were doing it correctly, checked we were enjoying it and then left us to it. Just before we had finished the Lagavulin, she was back with the Balvenie, informing us that we will have never drawn as much flavour from a Balvenie as we would when we were ready to drink this one. After we were done she was back again. We never had to wait for her, never had to try to find her. She wasn't serving a drink, she was delivering a full experience, one that was as reliant on timing and her attention as it was on the drinks in the glass.

She wasn't serving a drink, she was delivering a full experience, one that was as reliant on timing and her attention as it was on the drinks in the glass.

Both Dave and I felt it was one of the most memorable and unique whisky-drinking experiences that we had ever encountered. And as you may imagine, we told many people about it.

Same place, different experience

About two weeks later a couple of friends decided to act on my recommendation and go and try it for themselves. Like us they arrived at the restaurant, were greeted at the door, were shown to a table in the bar and left to peruse their menus. A few minutes later a woman approached their table to take their order; it was a different woman! It went a little something like this:

Her: 'You ready to order?'

Them: 'Yes, we would like two Speylay Explosions, please.'

Her: 'Eh?'

Them: Two Speylay Explosions, please'.

Her: 'Never heard of them.'

Them: [Slightly thrown by her response] 'Err, well, it's the one with the palate cleanser, followed by a Lagavulin accompanied by some dark chocolate—'

Her: [Interrupting them] 'For a start, they are two different drinks. You can have two if you want. And the chocolate isn't available to order, we give it to you as a gesture, if we have any.'

Them: [Deflated] 'Oh! Well, do you have any?'

Her: 'I'll check. Anything else?'

Them: [Losing interest now] 'Ermm, yes, a couple of shots of Balvenie Doublewood to finish.'

Her: 'Anything else?'

Them: 'That's it!'

The drinks were delivered, in silence, all together. No theatre, no personality, no care, instruction, ritual or attention. The chocolate came but it may as well have not been there. And eventually, when they got the bill, they felt overcharged for three drinks that they would never have ordered together and that they didn't enjoy at all.

It's all about the service

You see, my most memorable whisky-drinking experience wasn't about the drinks, it wasn't about the venue, or the company, or the chocolate. It was all about the young woman. She was amazing. She had essentially sold us three drinks each when we were only thinking about one. However, she packaged and presented her offering with passion, enthusiasm and expression. She had completely read our situation and tailored her level of service to our age, state of mind, time of day/week. It was exactly what we needed. In fact, it was far beyond anything I could have expected. The idea of selling us a three-drink combination as a fully encompassing drinking experience was completely inspired. And the level of attention and personalisation that she delivered throughout the whole experience made it stand out from any service experience I have received, either before or since.

> She had completely read our situation and tailored her level of service to our age, state of mind, time of day/week.

In fact, she delivered an experience so memorable that I have shared this story with thousands of bartenders ever since. It forms the basis of my case for developing skills and tailoring the service experience. Our eventual bill wasn't cheap but it was amazing value for money. So much so that I would have paid double. In fact, that is more or less what I did. I left a tip that represented approximately 60 per cent of the bill, the biggest tip in terms of a percentage that I have ever left anyone. Why? Because she was amazing, so skilled, so talented and so natural. There was a sense that she got as much pleasure from delivering mind-blowing service experiences for her guests as the guests did themselves. And of course, having done so, the power of reciprocity (the need to repay the deed) compelled me to tip her highly. Something that I took pleasure in doing.

In fact, if you take a look back through this story, you will notice that she used, to some degree, practically every skill we have covered in this book. And while she didn't work on the bar, she was the ultimate Ultimate Bartender writ large.

So, this is it, the start of your transformative journey. Consider this book your guide, a guide along the path to success. By having read it you can consider yourself as having taken the most difficult step of all towards change... The first one! You now have momentum, you have broken that point of inertia and have started to move in the right direction. How long your journey will take is in some respect dependent upon your desire for change, your hunger for improvement and the strength of your

commitment. But always remember that to become a true
Ultimate Bartender you will also need to realise that your
journey has no end. The decision to become an Ultimate
Bartender is a decision to adopt a philosophy that will shape
your career from this moment forward.

This book is not so much a definitive guide but rather a portal to
another world, the world of the Ultimate Bartender. By reading
the book you have opened that portal and taken a look at what's
on the other side. Having seen what's there you can never 'unsee'
it. Your view of what's possible and what you can achieve has
changed for ever, there is no going back; the only way is onwards
and upwards along your path to bartending greatness. So, pick a
skill, give it a go, learn from your mistakes and continue to
persevere. In time, and with dedication, your path to becoming
an Ultimate Bartender is assured. The only thing that can stop
you now is yourself.

Index

2 vs 1 serving technique 41–52
'7%-38%-55% rule' 126–33

actors
    thinking like 149–51, 159
    see also performance, bartender; show, the
age groups 98–9
Always be Learning (ABL) mindset 17–31
anxious guests 63, 81–2, 84, 87, 91–3
arrogance 176–8
'attitude to serve' xiv, 73–80
attributes of good bartenders 33–4, 35–9
awards 28

Bacardi 12–13
Bacardi Brown-Forman 110
Balvenie 64, 184–6
bar visits 29
beverage napkins 8
body language 130–3
Bolt, Usain 177
building drinks 12–13
busy bars 81–95, 143–60
'buzz-sessions' 113–14

challenges 79, 81–95, 143–60, 161–8
characteristics of good bartenders 33–4, 35–9
chilling drinks 10, 11
Cocktail (1988) 178
cocktails 4, 9–14, 25–6, 99–100
colleagues
    learning from 22–3
    recognition 28
    see also team-work
comfort zones, stepping out of 78
commonality 38
'communication conflict' 130–2
communication skills xiii–xv, 75
    and dress sense 175
    and engaging with guests xiv–xv, 2, 21–41,
        45, 47
    and 'Heads-Up' bartending 87–90
    and influencing guest decision-making 21–41
    non-verbal 126, 130–3

productive communication 127–30
    and recommendations 132–4
    verbal 126–33
competition 28
complacency 79
confidence 176–8
connected selling 65–6
consistency 3
consolidation 25–6
control, taking 97–107
cosmopolitan (cocktail) 10
cross-selling 66
Cruise, Tom 178

days of the week 101–2
decision-making
    influencing 21–41
    making things simple 67
Diageo 110
difficult guests 143–60
diluting drinks 10, 11
direct selling 64–5
Disneyland 30
distillery visits 26–7
'double-up for a pound' approach 55
dress sense 175
drink-making skills 1–6, 9–14, 46–50

EDIC (Explain, Demonstrate, Imitate,
    Consolidate) 25
egos 33, 35, 37, 176
emotional responses 122–5
empathy xiii, xv, 151–9
engaging with guests xiv–xv, 2, 21–41, 45, 47
entertainment factor 2, 45–6
expectations, guests' xiv, 53–72, 138–40
experiential learning 115–17
extras 7–9
eye contact xiv, 91

failure, embracing 78–9
flair bartending 178–9
flexibility 74–6
Ford, Henry 126

foundations of bartending 1–14
future, worrying about 162–4

garnishes 5–6, 8, 49
geekism 117–18
gender issues 99
gin 67, 112–14
gin and tonic 4, 7–9, 12, 43–4, 46–8
giving, receiving through 37
glassware
    handling 171–2
    high quality 4, 8
goal-setting x–xiii, 24–6, 28–9, 34–5
Gordon's 7
groups
    size 99–100
    types 100–1
guest interactions, reviewing your 23–4
guests
    age 98–9
    anxious 63, 81–2, 84, 87, 91–3
    dress style 105
    emotional responses 122–5
    engaging with xiv–xv, 2, 21–41, 45, 47
    expectations xiv, 53–72, 138–40
    gender 99
    happiness/satisfaction 34–5, 44–6, 73–4, 145
    loyalty 70, 140, 146
    needs 68
    not feeling noticed/feeling ignored 63,
        81–2, 84, 91–2
    reading 97–107
Guinness 105

hands, weak 49–51
Harrods 30
'Heads-Up' bartenders 81–95
humour xiii

ice 5
incentives 28
influencing techniques xiv, 21–41
'It's all in the Mind' 161–8
'It's Never Personal' mindset 143–60
'It's not what you say, it's the way you say it
    (and project it)' 127–30

jiggers 49–50, 172–3
Jobs, Steve 126

Kennedy, John F. 126
King, Martin Luther 126
knowledge, bartender 109–20

Lagavulin 184–5, 186
learning
    Always be Learning (ABL) mindset 17–31
    experiential learning 115–17
    learning cultures 28
    motivation for learning 27
    opportunities for learning 20–30
    product knowledge 109–20
    setting daily goals 28–9
Lewis, Carl 177
limbic system 123–5, 132–3
liquidation 59
listening skills 68, 127, 157–8
long-term thinking 68–70
luck 53

M&S food 133
Mandela, Nelson 126
manhattans (cocktails) 11
margaritas (cocktails) 25–6
martinis (cocktails) 4, 11
Mastermind (TV quiz show) 17–19
Mehrabian, Albert 125–6, 130, 132–3
Mental Health Foundation 161–2
message boards (online) 27
mint 12–13
mixing
    cocktails 9–14, 49–50
    spirits and mixers 46–9
mojitos (cocktails) 12–13
motivation, to learn 27

new experiences, willingness to try xiv, 70–1,
    101–2, 105
non-verbal communication 126, 130–3
now, power of 165–7

occasions, special 104–5
'one trick ponies' 76
one-handed service process 43–6
one-hour cocktail speed mix 42–3
online groups, joining 27
opportunities for learning 20–30
opportunity, sound of 56–7, 60, 63–4, 71
opportunity mindset 53–4, 56–71, 118–19, 134

'people businesses' 36
people skills xiii–xv, 35–9, 73–80, 75
    empathy xiii, xv, 151–9
    engaging with guests xiv–xv, 2, 21–41, 45, 47
    eye contact xiv, 91
    rapport-building xiii, xiv, 38–9, 46, 67, 69,
        75, 151, 157–9

relationship building 35–6
see also communication skills
perception
of quality 4, 7–8
of what is achievable viii–xiii
performance, bartender 169–80
see also actors; show, the
perseverance 79
personalised service 67, 69, 97–107, 135, 138–9, 179
personality types 76–8
perspective 164–5
Pimm's No. 1 102–3
positivity 92–3, 121, 125, 133–5, 138, 143, 146, 148, 159, 167, 181
posture 171
pouring 172–3
practical skills 1–6, 9–14, 46–50
premium products, upselling 64–5
present moment, being in the 165–7
prioritising guests 93
proactivity 97
producer visits 115–17
product knowledge 109–20
productive communication 127–30
productivity 41–52
pushy service 67

quality perception 2, 4, 7–8
queuing systems 88

rapport-building xiii, xiv, 38–9, 46, 67, 69, 75, 151, 157–9
reading guests 97–107
receptive communication 127
reciprocity 36–8, 134–7
recommendation-making 64–71, 74–5, 100–1, 132–4, 139–40
relationship building 35–6
reviews, of guest interactions 23–4
road-rage 152–4
rum 12–13

St Patrick's Day 105
'scanning' technique 62, 63, 93
seasons 102–4
second serve opportunities 59–63
self-analysis 23–4
self-development 110–13
self-interest model 135
selling 64–6
see also upselling

'Selling the Sizzle' 121, 122–3
serve, the 3–7
2 vs 1 41–52
one-handed service process 43–6
service attitude xiv, 73–80
service lessons, from other industries 29–30
shaking 173–4
show, the 181–9
see also actors; performance, bartender
skills sessions, running your own 23, 27
soda 12–13
special offers 55, 59–60
speed of operation, and the 2 vs 1 serving technique 41–52
stance 171
'stick-in-the-muds' 118–19
stirring 11–12
straws 8, 49
stress xv, 81–95, 143, 161–8
style 169–80
sugar 12–13

team-work 33–40, 169, 175–6
see also colleagues
'tells', showing 41–3
theatre of bartending 169–80
see also actors; show, the
time of day 101
timing issues 61–3, 101–2
tips 138–9, 140, 188
Tolle, Eckhart, The Power of NOW 166
training courses 20–2
training materials 28
training organisations 110
trust-building 67, 69, 140, 151, 157–9

upselling 30, 53–72, 74–5

Vadrna, Stanislav 173–4
value for money 4
verbal communication 126–33
vodka 58
voice 127–30, 132–3

waitresses, ultimate 183–8
'what can I do to make you happy?' mindset 36, 74
'what can you do for me?' attitudes 36
whisky 18–19, 65, 123, 132–3, 183–7
words 127–30, 132
work stress xv, 81–95, 143, 161–8
Wright, Bill 17–18